MW01200357

Ruffles and Lace

Julia~

Hope you enjoy!
the Book!

Ruffles and Lace

A SOUTHERN LADY'S JOURNEY IN BUSINESS AND FASHION DESIGN

Charles E. Cabler

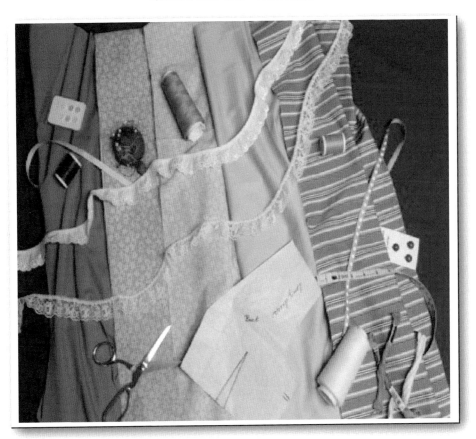

Author Charles E. Cabler

© July 2016
All rights are reserved. No part of this book may be copied, or reproduced by any means without the written permission from the author, except for brief quotations or review comments.

ISBN-10- 153554029X
ISBN-13- 9781535540292
Library of Congress Control Number: 2016912436
CreateSpace Independent Publishing Platform
North Charleston, South Carolina

Title page photo designed by Glenda L. Cabler and Debbie Johnson May
Title page photography by April Adams
Back cover photography by Debbie Johnson May

Disclaimer

THIS BOOK IS PUBLISHED SOLELY for information and entertainment purposes. While best efforts for accuracy have been used in writing this book, the author, book subject and publisher make no representations or warranties of any kind and assume no liabilities of any kind with respect to the completeness of the contents. Neither the author, book subject, nor the publisher shall be held liable or responsible to any person or entity with respect to any consequential damages caused, or alleged to have been caused, directly or indirectly, by the information contained herein.

"You can only become truly accomplished at something you love. Don't make money your goal. Instead, pursue the things you love doing, and then do them so well people can't take their eyes off you."

Maya Angelou

Dedicated To My Family

Genett H. Johnson

THE POTENTIAL FOR SUCCESS INCREASES when you have the right relationship with God and the love and support of family. I first thank God for the talent he gave me, and the things he has allowed me to do. For keeping me healthy, and blessing me with a wonderful family. Without Him, I could do nothing.

Secondly I thank my family. Members of a family are generally supportive of each other's endeavors, and my family has gone well beyond the expected in so many ways, and with so much love. It is difficult to find the right words to adequately convey my appreciation or demonstrate my gratefulness for all their devotion. It is with a deep sense of gratitude I express thanks to my family for their support and encouragement over these many years.

With love and affection I dedicate this book to:

Bill, my husband of sixty-three years, and his patience with me in all the things I have done. I could not have a better life-partner.

Debbie, my daughter, for being my very best friend, my inspiration and model.

Bill Jr., my son, for his love and the attention he has always given to please me.

Table of Contents

Forward

Debbie Johnson May

A Mom's Hug Lasts Long After She Lets Go

ALL WRITTEN WORDS ARE INTENDED to help us tell a story . . . perhaps about us, perhaps about someone else. This book does a little of both. I have known Charles Cabler literally since birth because his mother, Mary Lee, and my mother, Genett, are sisters. When I was a child, Aunt Mary Lee and Uncle Edd's home on Chisholm Road in Florence, Alabama was like my second residence. I spent many days at their house and have fond memories of time spent with my cousins.

Because of my dad's career, my family moved away from Florence when I was one year old and did not return to live there again until the early 1970s. Charles also left Florence, going into the military and pursuing his career in banking, before also returning "home" in 2015. During those years we seldom had contact, but life has a way of coming full circle and has brought us together once again.

I suppose people don't consider their parents' lives as anything but an extension of their own until adulthood. As I matured I realized my mother's life had been interesting, but even so, until some of the highlights were put on paper, I still didn't think of it as especially remarkable. Charles's words changed that. With a few strokes of his pen and words typed on a page, he brought the eighty-two years of one woman's existence to life – and has shared an incredible story.

My mother's mother, Mamaw to me, sewed beautifully and instilled a love of pretty clothes in Mother, which she passed on to me. (That's never changed!) She was Mother's teacher and inspiration, but Mother's talent and her abilities managed to surpass even Mamaw's.

Growing up, Mother was a "stay-at-home" mom to my brother, Bill, and me. She didn't work outside the home until I was in high school, so she taught me everything I know about being a wife and mother as I grew up. I remember the years when I wanted "store-bought" dresses. We'd go shopping, then she'd come home and make replicas of the dresses I wanted – the only difference was they always looked better than the ones in the store. Friends would ask over and over where we shopped, and I'd just smile.

Naturally, I took Home Economics in high school, but my sewing attempts never lived up to Mother's, so I cajoled her into making my clothes for many years. When my grandchildren came along, Mother's sewing was all about them, so I had to take a back seat – her first love was always making children's clothes. Of course, my grandchildren have been perfect models and loads of inspiration for her.

From her childhood in Florence to our travels throughout the country because of my father's career with the Treasury Department, to their return to their hometown, Mother kept the home fires burning and created a safe haven and beautiful environment for our family. She made life look easy in everything she did, even though I know that wasn't always the case. Like all of us, she had dreams – and she managed to make lots of them come true.

My mother is Mae Genett Herston Johnson–called Genett by the world–Genett with a G. She has been a daughter, sister, niece, cousin, aunt, employee, wife, mother, business owner, mother-in-law, entrepreneur, grandmother, great-grandmother, and friend.

Thank you, Charles, for writing an account of this special lady's life. I hope everyone enjoys her story. I know I'm one proud daughter!

Introduction

Charles E. Cabler

Turning Cant's into Cans and Dreams into Plans

THIS IS A STORY OF A YOUNG GIRLS interest in sewing and her visionary ability to design and create children's clothing patterns. It is an entrepreneur success story of a sewing talent turned into a business filled with opportunities, frustrations, unexpected events, and tremendous personal and professional success. Her personal story begins in 1974 as her sewing passion evolves into ownership of a fabric shop and eventually into designing patterns for children's clothing. This is a business story which continues today with a creative vision and vivid imagination.

The principal of this story is Mrs. Genett H. Johnson, managing partner of Ruffles and Lace Treasured Collection designs. Genett is not only an accomplished seamstress, but an acclaimed fashion designer, teacher and astute businesswoman. In 1974, Genett decided to expand her sewing interests and purchased a fabric shop in Florence, Alabama named Style Rite Fabrics, recognized for selling high quality fabric and sewing accessories. She owned and managed this shop for the next sixteen years.

In addition to owning the fabric shop, during the past thirty-five years, Genett and her business partner, Anita Jaynes, have become prominent children's clothing fashion designers for McCall's Patterns under the business name "Ruffles and Lace." As of this writing, more than one million Ruffles and Lace patterns have been sold across the United States and in many other countries.

Genett has received very few personal accolades for the significant contributions she has made to children's fashions. Other than a local news paper article or two over the years, and a McCall's catalogue article, she has received very little local recognition or promotion. In fact, many people in Florence have no idea of her accomplishments. In most probabilities, most seamstresses will never know the patterns they've used were created by Genett and Anita.

I take great pride in writing this book because Genett is my aunt, my mother's youngest sister. Although we both grew up in Florence, there is ten years difference in our ages, and therefore Genett and I had very little interaction. After graduating Florence State University, Genett's husband Bill, accepted an assignment in Raleigh, North Carolina and they moved away from Florence in 1955, not returning until 1973 to care for aging parents and relatives. I left Florence in 1972 to pursue a career in banking and our lives did not reconnect until 2015 after I retired and returned to Florence.

On a recent visit with Aunt Genett, we talked about our past experiences and I discovered the extent of her success story. Until that visit, I had no idea of her creative and entrepreneurial successes. We started a conversation about her life as a children's clothing designer, which fascinated me and was a story I thought should be told. After some discussion, we decided to collaborate and write this book in recognition of her work and success in her Style Rite Fabrics Shop and her design business Ruffles and Lace.

This inspiring story relating the power of her creativity, determination, resilience and commitment to her life's principles to achieve financial prosperity may surprise you. Her accomplishments in redefining children's clothing designs will fascinate you, and her dedication to raise funds to help eradicate breast cancer will make you appreciate her.

Because parts of this story took place some forty-three years ago, we've used Aunt Genett's best recollections to convey specific events and conversations with our intention to present these in a fair and entertaining way. Although Aunt Genett's memory is amazing and she recalls events and people with a good deal of clarity, I've invoked my artistic license to recreate some dialogue and compositionally embellish for the purpose of story continuity but always in the spirit of accuracy. Any actual or perceived misrepresentation of anyone or event contained in this book is unintentional.

This story also incorporates personal information contributed by Anita Jaynes, Genett's co- designer and Ruffles and Lace business partner, in addition to information extracted from published newspaper, magazine articles, and public information as reflected on the Information and Reference page. Reprints of patterns are used with the permission of the McCall's Pattern Company.

CHAPTER 1

My Family History

Genett H. Johnson

Where life begins and love never ends

GENETT'S HOME TOWN OF FLORENCE, ALABAMA, is a charming small southern city situated in the northwest corner of the state in Lauderdale County with the Tennessee River flowing through it. The cities of Sheffield, Tuscumbia and Muscle Shoals across the river in Colbert County adjoin Florence and collectively these four cities are referred to as "The Shoals."

Incorporated in 1826, Florence was surveyed for the Cypress Land Company by Italian surveyor Ferdinand Sannoner. He named it Florence after his home, the Capital of the Tuscany region of Italy, a city with which he was most familiar. As one of Tuscany's largest cities, Florence lies on the banks of the River Arno and is known for its lush landscapes, traditions, history, artistic legacy and its influence as a tourist destination. Considering Florence, Alabama's progress and development since 1826, it appears Mr. Sannoner was very accurate in his choice of names.

Genett begins her story, "The sixth of seven children, I was born in 1934. My family's heritage in Florence dates back to 1841 and is rich in southern history and tradition. My great grandfather on my dad's side served in the 27th Regiment, Alabama Infantry of the Confederate Army, and on my mother's side, military service includes a captain in the Revolutionary War. Some of the family owned and farmed plantation size tracts of land while others lived in town and were businessmen, preachers, home builders and millers.

We lived on a farm in Lauderdale County for several years. Daddy was a sharecropper and the house we lived in was part of his compensation. Mama worked at home doing all the customary family chores and helped Daddy in the field as needed. She tended our garden, milked the cows and churned butter. Best I remember, life was difficult and filled with hard work.

Our house was located close to the little Cypress Creek, and that was so memorable because my brothers were permitted to go swimming, but not me. Mama said I could not go swimming until I knew how to swim. I remember thinking, "How can I learn to swim if I can't go to the creek? Didn't make any sense to me, but what did I know, I was just a child. So, I swung on the tire swing in the front yard and made my play house on the ground under a big oak tree by placing rocks in line to make separate rooms. I had fun even if I couldn't go swimming.

Much to my dislike I had long hair down to my waist and Mama refused to cut it. It was so much trouble to keep clean and combed and hot in the summertime, I wished I had short hair like many of my girlfriends, but wishing was as far as I got. One day Daddy took me to town with him, while Mama stayed home. I realized this was my opportunity and begged Daddy to let me go to the beauty shop while we were in town. I think he was mad at Mama that day so, he gave me permission. The lady cut my hair just below my ears in a page boy style, and I was so happy. Needless to say Mama did not share in my joy and excitement. She stayed mad at me and Daddy for ever so long, but eventually she got over her mad spell, things returned to normal and I enjoyed my short hair immensely.

One of the most interesting places we lived was the Forks of Cypress. I was five years old and much too young to know and understand the historical significance of this grand old structure. If I did know, it probably didn't make any difference to me. It was our home, a place to be warm, eat, and sleep. But this historic old house was much more important than I realized at that time. There was another family living in the log cabin behind our house which was once occupied by slaves."

The Forks of Cypress

Main House   Log cabin-rear of main house

The Forks of Cypress was a plantation home designed by architect William Nichols for James Jackson and his wife, Sally Moore Jackson. James, one of the first settlers in Lauderdale County, was a distant relative and close friend of President Andrew Jackson. History indicates that President Jackson purchased land in Lauderdale County at the first public land sale in July, 1818. Local legend has it that President Jackson was a frequent visitor at the Forks of Cypress. The construction was completed in 1830, and it was the only Greek revival home in Alabama to feature a two-story colonnade around the entire house, composed of twenty-four Ionic columns. Genett says, "I remember hiding behind a column and jumping out to frighten Granny Williams, who lived with us. Granny didn't appreciate that, be we thought it was fun." The name, Forks of Cypress, was derived from the fact that Big Cypress Creek and Little Cypress Creek border the plantation and converge near the site of the main house. Tradition says James purchased the land from Chief Double Head, chief of the local Cherokee Indian tribe, who was given the land by the U.S. Government as part of his agreement to stop fighting.

James Jackson was quite an equestrian and in the 1820s and 30s, imported a dozen or more English thoroughbred horses for breeding with his own horses in an effort to improve the overall bloodstock of the American thoroughbred. He was eminently successful in his effort. The backside of the house had a walk-in basement, where James kept his horses during bad weather or for protection when needed.

James, who died in August 1840, was buried in the family cemetery near the home, and Sarah Jackson, James's widow, became the owner of the plantation. During the American Civil War invading Union forces used the lands of the Forks as a base camp, with no destruction of the home or other buildings. Additionally, some of Alex Haley's ancestors, including his grandmother, were slaves on this plantation, which provides a setting for much of his book, *Queen: The Story of an American Family.* In the 1950's the Forks was renovated, furnished with period antiques and guided tours of the house were given on the weekends. It was truly a grand southern plantation home. Unfortunately, lightning struck the Forks of Cypress home on June 6th, 1966 (6/6/66) and the entire home burned to the ground leaving only the twenty-four columns intact. The site was placed on the Alabama Register of Landmarks and Heritage in 1992 and on the National Register of Historic Places in 1997.

"The Rufus B. Dowdy family owned the Forks when we lived there and Daddy and several other men worked as sharecroppers. My older sister, Mary, and her husband, Edd rented two rooms on the second floor, and Edd worked for Mr. Dowdy clearing crop land for fifty cents per day.

One Christmas Santa came to the house all dressed in his red and white suit and scared me and my younger brother so bad, we hid under the bed. Santa left a doll and a toy car for us for our Christmas presents. Daddy never told us who Santa was, or if he had initiated the visit. Even in one of my last conversations with Daddy, he did not tell me. I just know that Santa came to our house that night.

Sharecropping became more difficult each year so, we moved from the farm into the city in 1943 when I was about nine years old. Daddy was a painter by trade and as with most construction trades, his income was dependent upon an economy where new homes were built, or where people had the money to paint their home. Mama found part time work at a local grocery shop and finally a full time job at the J.T. Flagg Knitting Mill in Florence.

Our family was just an average family on the block making it from paycheck to paycheck with every family member expected to do his or her part.

I grew up in a household where I learned the principles and benefits of hard work.

Life was difficult for my family and many other southern families in the 1940-1950 time frames. Employment opportunities were limited in the small city of Florence and the pay was often low for the available jobs. Mama's full time job at the knitting mill paid a gross annual salary of $2,042 in 1951.

Needless to say, the requirement to cut corners in the budget at every opportunity was a daily event for us. For men in the family having a small garden was essential and hunting was both a sport as well as a way to put meat on the table. For women in the family, sewing, quilting, knitting and crocheting were not only pastimes but necessities

Working together, we survived some very difficult years, and I learned many practical lessons during the survival process. I often take time to reflect on my life and the many positive results of those difficult years."

CHAPTER 2

Remembering Mama's Influence

There is nothing like Mama's attention

RECALLING THE EARLIEST MEMORY of her mother's sewing influence, Genett says. "It is difficult to remember a time when sewing was not a significant part of my life. From my earliest memory of helping Mama as a young girl of nine years old to today as I continue to sew for my great-grandchildren, sewing has been a prominent life element. Sewing has always been more than just a hobby for me, it has been a passion with a desire to excel, and my sewing knowledge and skills have proved useful in many ways over the years.

As a young family just starting our life on Bill's first Department of the Treasury assignment in Raleigh, North Carolina, cost counting expenses was very necessary. Purchasing children's clothing was not a line item in our budget. Necessities like socks and shoes had to be bought, but I made most of the clothing for me and my daughter saving us a tremendous amount. If I do say so myself, my little daughter was one of the best dressed girls in her class.

I attribute my success in great part to my Mother who helped to formulate my interest in sewing and instilled in me the aspiration to become a good seamstress. Mama was very proficient in her sewing skill and without that, our family would not have been blessed with the clothing we wore. I can remember wanting to be with Mama when she sewed, especially if she was making something for me. I thought it fascinating that she knew just how to cut the pieces of material, sew them together and make a beautiful dress, skirt or blouse. I recall thinking, "I want to learn how to do that one day."

Although patterns were available for women's clothing, finding a suitable pattern for a little girl's dress was almost impossible, and Mama usually did not like those which were available. Rather than settle for a pattern she did not like, she made her own patterns. She had a vision how she wanted the garment to look so; using an old newspaper or even a brown grocery bag, she made her own pattern. She would lay the paper against my chest or back, measure and mark before cutting it. She would determine the type collar and sleeves she wanted, measure, design and cut them also.   Mama always made me such pretty dresses, skirts and blouses. They were unlike anything in the department stores, and my girlfriends were so envious of me. They often wanted to borrow my clothes, as we did back in those days, and I would caution them not to tear or get holes in them. They knew that if that occurred, there would be no more borrowing from me.

It always amazed me how Mama could make a dress out of such a small amount of material. When she finished cutting out all the pieces, there was very little material left over. Mama never threw anything useable away, a practice I learned from her and still find myself replicating today even though everything is much more assessable. She saved pieces of material too small to make a garment but that perhaps could be used for a collar or sleeves on another garment. Even smaller pieces were saved and used to make a quilt top.

Nothing went to waste. When a garment wore out, Mama would keep anything still useful: the zipper, buttons, cuffs and collars were reused on a future garments. This practice was considered thrifty during those years, but in today's clothing, it is fashionable. The worn out denim look is frequently used to accentuate several types of clothing, jackets and handbags. Today it's viewed as "chic." Mama was stylish back then and didn't even know it.

Electric sewing machines were available during those years, but Mama could not afford one. She used a standard Singer treadle type machine. In case you are not familiar with that terminology, it was a sewing machine operated by the foot to produce a reciprocating or rotary motion. On a treadle machine, the only way the needle moves up and down is a continual motion of pressing down on the foot treadle. When you stopped pushing the treadle, the sewing stopped. I remember sitting at Mama's feet and pressing the treadle after Mama's legs grew so tired she could no longer push. I was always anxious for her to stop long enough to get another piece of material because that gave me a temporary rest also. I still have Mama's old Singer treadle machine, and each time I pass by it, I have fond memories of her sewing a dress for me."

The invention of the treadle machine in 1755 was a major advancement in making clothing. Until then, all clothing was made by hand a tedious and labor intensive process not to mention the sore fingers and hands. While a hand sewn dress or shirt might take up to fourteen hours, the treadle sewing machine reduced that time down to two to three hours, depending on the complexity of the garment. It was an innovative solution to a tedious process.

Sewing was a skill, which was passed down from mothers to daughters for many generations. Genett states, "My mother acquired the skill from my grandmother, and passed it along to me. By the time I was old enough to learn how to sew my two older sisters were already married with their own home, so Mama had a lot more time to spend with me. Mama taught me how to lay out a pattern and cut the material without any waste. She showed me many tricks and shortcuts in making a garment, and believe me, these shortcuts were not taught in home economics class. They were learned only after many years of sewing experience.

But my opportunities to learn to sew were somewhat limited. To sew, you must have material, thread, buttons, and trim. Money was needed to purchase them, and as I previously stated, money around our house was always scarce. Going to a fabric store to purchase material was almost out of the question because of the expense involved. Why, to buy enough material, thread, and buttons to make a dress would cost three to four dollars. That was an unheard expense in our family, so it was always a treat when Mama had enough money to buy material.

Most of my dresses were made using flour sacks. Many companies would package their flour, meal or sugar in cotton bags printed with colorful flowers or small designs. Mama used those cotton sacks to make me a dress. When Daddy went to the grocery store, Mama would remind him to bring back two sacks of flour or meal that matched in color or design, because most dresses required two sacks to have enough material.

When the sack was empty, Mama would wash it, fold it carefully and place it in her material drawer to keep for a future sewing project. When Mama finished my dress, it was as pretty as any dress bought at a department store, and I wore it proudly.

My first sewing assignment from Mama was an apron. I laid out the pattern, carefully cut it out and sewed it together. I was elated that I had done so well on my first try. Mama inspected it and complimented me on a good job, then gave my next assignment, a dress. Oh my! That was certainly a big leap for such a young seamstress. Dress patterns back then were rather simple with a two piece top sewed together and attached to a gathered skirt. The sleeves and collar were attached after the basic parts were sewn together.

Once again I carefully laid out the pattern on the material taking time to precisely cut each piece. I sewed them together and tried it on so Mama could mark the skirt length. To my great surprise the dress was too big on me. "How'd that happen?" I was smaller than the pattern size and either Mama did not tell me to reduce the pattern size, or I didn't listen to Mama's instructions. Never the less, the dress was way too big! It just hung on my small frame. I was so disappointed that my results were not as good as the apron, and was ready to give up and quit.

"Oh no" said Mama. "That is not the way we sew. Take it apart and let's see how much we need to cut it down." "That seemed like a lot of work to me, but I did as Mama instructed and took it apart. I was introduced to a new sewing tool called a 'seam ripper', and throughout my many years of sewing I have become very proficient with this tool.

Mama showed me how to reduce the pattern size to make it fit me, and it worked. I sewed it back together again. It was a very special dress and I wore it proudly knowing that I had made it. My first dress! That lesson of long ago still resonates with me each time I make a miscalculation putting patterns together to make something. Had it not been for Mama's insistence, I would not have learned a very valuable lesson. You will never out grow making mistakes, but you can usually correct them if you will take time."

That said however, even the most experienced seamstress is subject to mistakes which cannot be corrected. "I won't go into details about any of my uncorrectable mistakes but will share with you an example of one mistake made by my older sister, Mary Lee, an accomplished seamstress and a sewing perfectionist.

Mary did alterations of ready-to-wear clothing frequently because she would complete them quicker and more efficiently than the in-store alteration option. On one occasion she was asked to shorten the length of a pair of men's trousers for the son of a good customer. Mary took the measurements, cut one leg at the desired length ready to whip-stitch it for no cuff. Before she got to the other leg however, she was distracted for a short time before she returned to complete her project. The young man tried on the trousers to check the length, walked back into the sewing room and said, "I don't think this is correct." One leg was the original length and the other leg was cut off two inches too short. Inadvertently, my sister had cut the same trouser leg twice. Needless to say, Mary was embarrassed and devastated that she had ruined the young man's trousers." The seamstress and the carpenter share the same basic rule to measure twice, cut once. It always works!

I credit my success in great part to Mama and her patience and willingness to take time to teach me the proper and correct way to sew. I am certain it was a challenge for her at times, and I remember many of those lessons with great fondness. Even today while sewing I remember Mama's advice or instruction just like it was yesterday. Mama lived to see me become a successful seamstress, fabric shop owner and fashion designer, for which I am most thankful. I think she was proud of the seamstress she created."

CHAPTER 3

A Homemade Evolution

Genett Says Happiness Is Homemade

"MOST ALL OUR FAMILY CLOTHING was homemade out of whatever material was available at the time" Genett says. "Mama always tried to make clothes in appropriate style, design and color I would be proud to wear. That said however, if all Mama had for my brother's shirt was material with small flowers and leaves on it, there would always be a fight. I am sure my brother was ribbed incessantly about some shirts he wore, but his choice was wearing a new shirt or the old worn-out one, and often that was a no-brainer decision."

The term "homemade" is used affectionately and with respect because the concept of being "homemade" has changed dramatically over time. In years gone by all clothing was homemade because there was no other choice. I like the statement made by country singer Loretta Lynn in a recent magazine interview discussing some of her first performances, "When the times get tough, the tough get sewing. I only had two performance dresses, and back stage between sets, I would take the fringe off one dress, and then sew it on the other dress so I could go back onstage in a different color dress." However, sewing was a skill some women just could not master. Perhaps gifted with other skills, they were unable to follow a pattern design, thread a needle or grasp the concept of sewing material together. These women and their families still needed clothing and therefore resorted to hiring someone to custom make their clothing, thus the *seamstress* occupation was created.

The industrial revolution created the ability to increase production of many consumer goods giving birth to ready-to-wear clothing. For the wealthy, they no longer had to make their clothing, but enjoyed a wide variety of *ready-to-wear* clothing in differing styles and colors, which were immediately available. It was considered chic to name drop the department store as the place where the garment was purchased. That equated to boasting about the amount spent to make the purchase. "Homemade" became a concept of one's financial inability to purchase clothes off- the-rack.

With the mass produced ready-to-wear clothing so readily available, some women began to look for the not-so-available clothing to be distinguished in the crowd. It was considered an embarrassing moment to be seen in public wearing a garment the same as someone else. Therefore, the *fashion designer* began to be recognized as the way to acquire clothing much different from the ready-to-wear rack at the department store. This was a process, in which a designer was commissioned to create a pattern specifically for the garment and often specifically for the purchaser.

"I am a seamstress" Genett states, "however all my sewing has been confined to my family: dresses, skirts, blouses, shirts, sport coats and even wedding dresses. I have never been a seamstress for hire, although my older sister, Mary Lee, was. She was an excellent seamstress and usually had a long list of customers, many of whom would gladly wait for several weeks to get a custom made garment. She was a perfectionist and always produced a beautiful garment."

As in many creative efforts, mistakes are inherent within the sewing process, and even for professionals, attention to detail is an absolute necessity. Genett says, "I have made my share of mistakes and even lost my composure occasionally when I had to take a dress apart and re-sew it properly or remove a zipper I put in upside down. It is an aggravation, but necessary to have the garment look well. At about age fifteen, my older sister Mary was teaching me how to properly put in a zipper. As I stated in an earlier chapter, she was a perfectionist and often fastidious when it came to sewing, so the zipper had to be perfect. I took out and re-sewed that zipper seven times on the skirt she was using to teach me, before she said that's a good job. I got additional experience on the seam ripper, and I was never so happy to finally have that zipper in. I thought, perhaps next time I'll just use buttons."

"All garments begin with a concept, idea or vision which is then translated into a paper pattern. Often I knew what I wanted to make for a great-granddaughter, and how I wanted it to look. Unfortunately, I could not always find the pattern I needed. Sometimes I could put two or three different pattern pieces together to accomplish my objective, but more often that process did not work out satisfactorily. That frustrated me, so I decided I can make my own pattern, and I did. First one pattern then another until several dress patterns had been made."

Working as a fashion designer is difficult work. It is tedious, stressful and fraught with problems. If you do not have a significant degree of patience, you do not need to be in the fashion business. Genett says, "I am proud to refer to myself as a fashion designer because I really enjoy the challenges it presents, and the dresses I create. I did not set out to become a fashion designer. I just wanted to sew and make children's clothing for my family and grandchildren.

In fact, before we flew to New York to meet with McCall's, I was making one of my great-granddaughter's a dress to wear for her School's Fall Celebration Banquet. It was a beautiful combination of muted green and gold watercolor print with three quarter length puff sleeves, a caplet collar and French lace embellishment. A Ruffles and Lace design of course, and I was so proud to see her wear it. As most grandmothers, I am prejudiced when it comes to my family. I think they are the prettiest and wear the best looking clothes of anyone. Naturally, all Ruffles and Lace designs.

Just recently my seven year old great granddaughter Olivia, who has begun to develop an interest in sewing, said, "G.G. (the great-grand children's vernacular for great-grandmother) I want you to make me a white dress."

"Why do you need a white dress?" I asked.

"Cause I am going to a wedding," she replied.

"When is this wedding?" I inquired.

"Tomorrow," she said without hesitation.

"I had to laugh under my breath, as I told her I didn't have enough time to make her a dress. I am so delighted that she is interested in sewing and I intend to teach her everything she is willing to learn. Who knows, she may be the next family clothing designer."

"Unfortunately, I fear that home sewing is a dwindling art", as my partner Anita and I stated in a *Times Daily* newspaper interview. "It's such a shame there are people who can't even sew on a button. I've had people come into the shop and ask me to sew on a button for them" Anita added. Genett says "After you learn the basics, sewing is often something you can teach yourself. It takes a lot of practice and patience to do it right and unfortunately many people give up on learning."

So the evolution from homemade, to off-the-rack, to custom made, to fashion design, and back to homemade, has been completed. Although off-the-rack- clothing is convenient; there is something about the challenge to create your own dress that is self fulfilling. Perhaps mothers will continue to teach their daughters how to sew and the art will remain in place for years to come.

CHAPTER 4

Style Rite Fabrics Shop

Always buy fabric, no matter how much you already have.

GENETT CONTINUES, "SEWING FOR MY FAMILY and designing patterns as needed continued to encompass my world. My daughter and three granddaughters kept me busy most of the time with an occasional break to sew for myself. Even though sewing was enjoyable, it was not without its problems. There were a just a few stores in Florence which sold fabric and accessories, and it was not unusual for them to be out of the particular thing I wanted."

"We can order it for you" was the resolution I heard more often than not.

"I do not want to wait for it to be ordered. I want it- no, need it- now, right now!"

To be frugal with their operating budget, these fabric stores often carried a limited number of bolts of material in inventory. Instead they carried a lot of flat folds of varying amounts and you may, or may not, find enough material in the flat folds to make the garment you intended to make. "When Mama shopped at these stores, she often settled for whatever material was available. But contrary to Mama, I do not like to settle!"

"One day I went to one of these stores to buy lace for a dress I was making and needless to say, they were out and did not expect another shipment in until the following week. I drove home just frustrated. I thought to myself, "We need a fabric shop here that is more in touch with the needs of those who

15

sew. If that were my shop, I would make sure to keep a good stock of material and accessories."

Much to Genett's surprise, the opportunity to own that type shop came along shortly thereafter in 1974. Irvine Melicks and Sue Hammond had owned the fabric shop in North Florence for ten years, and both were ready to leave the retail business. Genett says, "I had been a customer of the shop since returning to Florence a year earlier, and found Style Rite Fabrics carried a better quality of everything. Irvine and Sue knew how insistent I was about having the right material and accessories to sew, so they approached me about purchasing the shop.

"You are always disappointed when you can't find everything you want," Sue said, "so this is a way you can do that and never be disappointed again."

"I know, I said, but buying material, a spool of thread, and a zipper is one thing, buying the whole shop is something else"

"It's not that much different" Irvine said, "You're just buying in larger amounts."

"Yeah, a lot larger amounts", I said and chuckled.

"Although I had a lot of experience putting the right material and accessories together to purchase, never in my wildest dream did I anticipate the opportunity to own a fabric shop. The thought of it scared me to death and purchasing the shop would certainly be a leap of faith."

"Let me think about it and discuss it with my husband, Bill" I said to them. "I will let you know in a few days.

Bill has always been supportive of me and having that type partnership is particularly important in a major decision such as this. Bill and I talked it over for several days discussing the pros and cons and decided that provided we could get the financing we needed, we would buy Style Rite Fabrics. If we could not get financing, that was God's way of telling us we should not buy.

Our financial situation was very solid, but we did not want to put our savings and investments at risk to make this purchase. We updated our financial statement, obtained the most recent Style Rite Fabrics operating and income statements from Irvine, and made an appointment with our banker. It was a productive meeting and within an hour we had access to the money we needed. We concluded God was making a way for us, and we would accept it.

We did make the purchase and Irvine offered to stay on during the transition until I understood how things worked. I really appreciated her willingness to do that. It made learning so much better because I had an experienced person to whom I could ask questions or seek advice when I needed it. She went with me to the Atlanta fabric market, introduced me to the fabric manufacturers' representatives, and showed me how to efficiently purchase fabric. We also made the rounds to the wholesale houses while we were in Atlanta and I gained a good understanding of inventory control and refreshed my bookkeeping skills from high school."

Style Rite Fabrics was far from the average fabric shop. It was a shop filled with upscale fine fabrics of cotton prints and solids, silks, georgettes, linens, satins and often, woolens, which you couldn't find everywhere. There was a great selection of trims including Swiss embroideries, eyelets, satin ribbons, and grosgrain ribbons in every color imaginable. A wide variety of other accessories and sewing notions including thread, buttons, appliqués, sequins, and zippers were just as plentiful. It was most unusual if a customer could not purchase and carry home everything needed for their garment. The goal of Style Rite Fabrics was to maximize the customers' sewing possibilities, and they did it well.

"I was so proud of my shop. I remember the first day I unlocked the door, stepped inside and looked around at all my merchandise. "This is all mine" I thought jubilantly. I can hardly believe it." Then just as quickly, I had a sinking feeling and a rhetorical question of, "What have I done?" Regaining my composure, I flipped on the lights, put the money in the register, started the coffee, and made ready for the day's activity.

My first customer was Mary Berry from Tennessee, a friend I previously met as a fellow Style Rite Fabrics customer. We saw each other from time to time during our shopping trips, and our friendship grew into a strong and lasting bond. When I told Mary of my plans to buy the shop she was excited. "I want to be your first customer" she said, "so tell me when your first day will be." Mary purchased dress material and accessories for all three of her daughters that first day. She continued to be a friend, a loyal Style Rite Fabrics customer, and I hired her as an employee some eight years later."

The Style Rite Fabrics shop was first located in a building on North Wood Plaza. God richly blessed Genett's business and after ten years of operation, she out grew that building. The lack of space, increasing rent, in addition to other reasons, prompted her to consider relocating. When a larger store came available in the Seven Points Shopping Center, she leased it. Being located in large shopping center provided ample pedestrian foot traffic. The store's two large front windows had an elevated stage-type floor providing the opportunity for displaying their dresses, and a separate framed, glass enclosed, display window was the perfect place to showcase the special of the week.

The shopping center was just a few blocks from the Wood Avenue Historical District residential area with its beautiful old Victorian, elaborate Queen Anne, and classic Georgian Revival style houses, most built between 1880 and 1930. Two plantation cottage style homes, built in the 1820's, are also on Wood Avenue. The beautiful old oak, hickory and popular trees which line Wood Avenue provide the neighborhood both beauty and shade. Contrary to many other areas in Florence, this neighborhood has experience very little changed since the early 1900's. Several notable residents who lived on Wood Avenue over the years include: Tom Stribling, a 1933 Pulitzer Prize winning author of the book, *The Store*; George Goethals, chief engineer of the Panama Canal; Helen Keller while attending public school; and Tom Rogers, founder of Rogers Department Store.

"I remember vividly my excitement as I closed the shop and locked up at the end of that first day. It was a good day's business, and I remember thinking as I drove home, "I know I can do this." I lived and breathed Style Rite Fabrics six days a week and remained passionate about my shop and work until the day I sold it sixteen years later."

CHAPTER 5

The Customer Comes First

Genett Says, Your Customers are Partners in Your Mission

DRAWING FROM HER OWN EXPERIENCE shopping at other stores, Genett understood the importance of providing good customer service. "Irvine and Sue, the previous owners, had made a good start in developing a good customer base, and I wanted to continue their work while creating a culture of valuing customers. It was my goal to make each customer feel welcome and important. I tried to live by a quote I once read, "People will forget what you said, and people will forget what you did, but people will never forget how you made them feel."

I am proud to say that my customers grew to depend on me to keep a good inventory stock to accommodate their needs. They often placed their specific material request with me before I went to the fabric market, and it was not unusual for many bolts of material to be sold from the backroom when they arrived from the manufacturer without ever seeing the retail floor.

To increase my customers' knowledge and sewing skills, I offered advanced sewing classes on special techniques such as French hand sewing or smocking. Jean Kirby, a good friend from Huntsville and an accomplished seamstress, conducted many of these classes using a Bernina brand sewing machine in her class."

Bernina, a Swiss company, produces high-end computerized sewing and embroidery systems. Bernina promotes itself to be at the cutting edge of technology and continues to be at the forefront of many of the major advances in sewing machine technology. Bernina is one of the better sewing machines, if not the best, as well as expensive, and does many time-saving stitch variations including embroidery and quilting. Genett says, "Because of Jean's demonstrations of this machine in her classes and the interest my customers had in purchasing a machine, I thought it advantageous to acquire the dealership charter for the Shoals area. I did and sold several machines during my ownership of Style Rite Fabrics.

Anita Jaynes was a dear friend of mine and loyal Style Rite Fabrics patron who purchased a significant amount of products during my ownership of the shop. She was also passionate about sewing, and we engaged in sewing conversations over coffee on several mornings, exchanging sewing ideas, disappointments and frustrations."

Anita's love of sewing came down through her family as did Genett's. Her grandmother made dresses for her five daughters and one of her great aunts was well known for her hand embroidered fine linens. Anita was also introduced to sewing through watching her mother make beautiful dresses, skirts, and blouses. As her enthusiasm grew, Anita said she became infatuated with the variety of fabric in the shop. There were so many design and color combinations, it was almost impossible to make a selection for one dress. She browsed through the pattern books with her mother to select just the right dress pattern, and then helped choose the buttons and other accessories. "How exciting was that?" she said. Each dress meant much more because she participated in the process. "Anita told me very proudly that the blouse making project in her high school home economics class turned out so well, she entered it in the 4-H Club sewing contest and won first prize. Way to go Anita!

"Anita was someone with whom I could share a sewing conversation, and it was refreshing to have Anita with me. She spoke the same language, and understood sewing problems and complexities. Anita also found it a challenge to locate patterns to her liking for children's clothing. We often collaborated on a particular pattern either she or I needed, and discovered we shared a lot of design interest.

My Style Rite Fabrics business had grown substantially and had reached the point where I needed part- time help. Not just a salesperson, but someone who appreciated the sewing challenges. Anita had demonstrated a genuine interest in the shop's success as well as pattern design and was looking for part-time work. So, it seemed that God had answered my prayer about finding a dependable person. After some discussion, I hired Anita as a part- time employee.

Anita and I worked well together and in 1981 we began to design and make our own children's dresses. We designed and made several dresses and displayed them in the shop, and they were received very well. Customers wanted one of our designed dresses for their daughters, so we developed a policy that if the customer purchased the material and all accessories from us, we gave them a copy of our hand-drawn pattern. That proved to be a great marketing tool. However, it did have a down side. Although it was a good way to sell our fabric and accessories, our designs were so much in demand, it was difficult to accommodate our customers' needs and questions. The patterns did not include directions, thereby creating a plethora of "how to" questions. Style Rite Fabrics was known for service and help, but sometimes the phone calls would almost be more than we could handle I said in an interview for a *McCall's* magazine article. What began as a way to increase sales and help our customers quickly escalated into a full scale project.

Additionally, we learned how to effectively market our products. For example, if a particular bolt of material was not selling well, I made a dress, skirt, or blouse and displayed it along with the bolt of material. We discovered that often people did not have a vision or concept about how a particular color or material design pattern would look, once made into a garment. This display technique proved to be very an effective sales effort.

My daughter, Debbie, worked part-time at Style Rite Fabrics for several years. Browsing around the shop, she often found a piece of material she liked and would, in her sweet way, coerce me into making her an outfit. Being a loving and accommodating mother, I would. One particular outfit I made was a sundress design with wide shoulder straps, fitted at the waist, and a gathered skirt with lace on the hem.   It really looked cute on her. She wore it to work one day and a young University of North Alabama (UNA) college student came in and fell in love with it. She had to have one just like it. Debbie showed her the material and encouraged her to make a dress for herself. Nothing doing. She could not sew and didn't want to learn how, but she wanted that dress.

"You want to sell that dress you are wearing?" the young student asked.

"Don't know, haven't given any thought about it," my daughter said.

The student made an offer to buy the dress, and my daughter said, "Sold." She went home, changed into another dress and returned to the shop. The student paid her for the dress and left a very happy customer. Talking about selling the clothes off your back. After that experience I assumed anything can and will happen in a fabric shop.

Anita and I continued to work together and our affinity in Style Rite Fabrics grew exponentially."

CHAPTER 6

The Start of Something Big

Genett Recalls a Visit from the McCall's Representative

DURING THE 1980s, IT WAS COMMOM PRACTICE for pattern and fabric manufactures to send representatives around the country making stops at wholesale and retail fabric shops to visit with the owners, thank them for carrying their merchandise in stock, and encourage them to continue. Among many others, representatives from Coats & Clark, Lily, La Mode Buttons, Robert Kaufman Fabrics, and McCall's Patterns regularly visited with Style Rite Fabrics to show their new fabric samples, thread, trim or notions, enticing an order. Bernina and Singer sewing machine manufactures also came by to demonstrate their latest machine and attachments. These representatives were the company's eyes and ears in the local fabric shops and a barometer of the public perception of their products.

Genett said, "We did not always place an order, but it made us feel good that these representatives thought enough of us and our shop to drop by. We and our shop were recognized as a player in the market, and we appreciated that.

One day Anita and I were having a cup of coffee discussing a particular design problem with one of our dress patterns when Bob Sellers, a representative from McCall's Pattern Company, came into the shop. Bob's purpose was to determine if we, and our customer's, were satisfied with their patterns, and if we had any suggestions. As a general rule, McCall's offers several hundred new designs in their annual catalogue and in addition to their pattern sales tracking capability, it was important for McCall's to understand the consumers perception of these patterns even if they are the dominate pattern company. These visits produce the type of information which seldom makes it to the CEO's office unless someone goes to the fabric stores and asks questions. Perception and acceptance are important descriptors of any company success, and McCall's knows that very well. Additionally, the McCall Pattern Company is diligent to send their representatives to the international trade and fashion shows to stay current on European designs because of the influence they have on American designs. Bob was courteous with a pleasant disposition and appeared to appreciate our views and opinions of McCall's patterns.

"Good morning, ladies" Bob said cheerfully and offered a charming smile.

"Just wanted to drop by to see how you, and your customers, like the selection in this year's pattern catalogue?"

Now, had Bob known the answer he was about to receive, perhaps he would have refrained from asking that particular question and instead focused on if Genett and Anita were enjoying the weather, or if their golf game was on par. But he didn't. The question was asked, very directly, and couldn't be retracted.

Genett says, "In my Southern culture, if you don't want an honest answer, don't ask the question. If you want an agreeable answer, phrase your question so it is easy to receive an agreeable answer. Since Bob asked a direct response question, I assumed he would appreciate an honest answer."

"I am not at all happy with the McCall patterns I carry in stock" I said "and, in fact, the patterns for little girl's dresses are very limited and, in my opinion, just not pretty at all." I was straight forward, and I took advantage of this opportunity to voice the frustrations Anita and I had harbored for some time."

Looking somewhat bewildered, Bob replied with a slight chuckle. "It is what it is and unfortunately there is nothing I can do about that, Mrs. Johnson."

"Oh yes there is," I said "Let me sell you some of our patterns. They are better than what you have to offer, and we sell more of our designs than any pattern in your book."

"If this trend continues," I added, "We may publish our own children's pattern catalogue."

With that remark, we got Bob's undivided attention. We offered him a cup of coffee and engaged in a conversation about what was good and not so good with McCall's patterns. We took the opportunity to let him know their patterns for children's clothing did not have the variety or styles needed to meet our customers' demands. We showed him several of our design dresses and told him about our marketing procedure to provide a copy of our pattern to anyone who purchased our products to make a dress. Bob thought that was a super marketing technique to increase sales. To say he was impressed would be an understatement.

Because he was not raised in the South, Bob was not at all in-tune with a mother's propensity to dress her daughter in ruffles and lace dresses. He seemed intrigued with this concept, and he readily admitted that McCall's had never concentrated on children's clothing to the same degree they focused on women's and men's clothing. At the conclusion of our conversation, he gave us a name and phone number for a McCall's contact in New York. He promised to share our design information with the designers at the home office to see if they had any interest in looking at them.

After several calls and messages, I finally received a call back from Robert L. Hermann, President and CEO of McCall Pattern Company. He was on his way to the Atlanta fabric market and asked if we could bring our sample dresses and meet him there. Based on the information Bob Sellers took back from his visit, Mr. Hermann indicated he definitely had an interest in our designs, and I agreed to meet with him.

When I returned to the sales floor and told Anita about the conversation, she was ecstatic."

"Oh my goodness, what a surprise," Anita said with a big smile on her face. "I never expected to hear from anyone, did you?"

"No I didn't," I replied "But this is great and maybe, a door of opportunity has opened for us. Now all we have to do is sell ourselves and our designs. Are you up to this?"

Anita replied, "You bet I am."

Anita, Gail Stephenson, and I drove to Atlanta the following day and went to the fabric market at the convention center. Now the fabric market in Atlanta is a big deal twice a year. Usually over one hundred manufacturers display the newest fabric and sewing accessories, and sewing machines and attachments for the upcoming season, so you can literally walk your legs off perusing all the merchandise. To have sufficient time, we drove to Atlanta on Wednesday and returned home on Sunday, a combination of purchasing for the shop and enjoying some of Atlanta's fine cuisine. We were always exhausted after five days of continuous activity.

We presented our sample dresses and discussed our design concepts with Mr. Hermann. Our children's dress designs were significantly different from the more traditional McCall dresses. Their patterns offered above the knee hemline dresses with collars, puffy sleeves, sashes and bows. Our frilly designs involved much more flare with plenty of ruffles, trim and lace. The type dress we visualized on a little Southern girl.

The more we talked, the more excited Mr. Hermann became. He was delighted with our designs and complimented us again and again on our work. He asked to take our ten sample dresses back to New York with him to in order to discuss the possibilities with his chief designers. We agreed to permit him to do so after he signed a receipt of acknowledgement and agreement not to replicate any design. We departed company, concluded our shopping, and returned to Florence.

As you would imagine, the ride home was filled with excitement and a little apprehension. It seemed as though we talked all the way home discussing many options and opportunities we may encounter and how they might affect us. We had a hundred questions running through our minds: *Was this for real? Is it possible that we could be designing for McCall's? Were we destined for success in the big market? Would our hopes and dreams be shattered? Did we just give away our designs?* Deep down, I think we both trusted Mr. Hermann and felt our designs were safe with him. In our excitement and apprehension we agreed to remain positive without any anticipation or expectation. We decided the Doris Day approach, Que Sera Sera ("whatever will be, will be") was in our best interest.

Several days passed without us hearing anything. We didn't talk about it for fear of jinxing our chances, and besides, if they were not interested, we did not want to be too disappointed. We kept this opportunity secret and did not mention it to any of our friends. Each time the phone rang at the shop we hoped it would be Mr. Hermann. Then one morning we received the phone call on which we were waiting. Mr. Hermann sounded excited and informed us the designers were so impressed with our dress designs they wanted to discuss including some of them in their spring catalogue, if we could come to an agreement.

"Can you fly to New York next week to meet with my staff and discuss a business arrangement?" Mr. Hermann asked.

"We certainly can." I replied.

"Great. I will have my Administrative Assistant make the arrangements, and be in touch with you." he said.

CHAPTER 7

Look Out New York, Here We Come

Stay calm and Love Fashion

THIS WAS THE FIRST TRIP to New York for Genett, Anita, and Gail. Genett said. "Just being in New York City was exciting, and added to that excitement our purpose for being there- meeting with the McCall Company- we were ecstatic. It was a dream come true and we could hardly contain our enthusiasm. Anita and I were there to represent our dress designs in this business transaction, and Gail, a good customer of Style Right and a design contributor was there to give us moral support and encouragement, in case we needed it. Three southern ladies had actually been invited to NYC by McCall's pattern company. Wow!

Our flight from the Huntsville airport was very early on a Tuesday morning, and we arrived at JFK International Airport still in time for breakfast. The freshly baked bagels and apple scones smelled so delicious, but unfortunately, the smell was all we had time for. We made our way to the baggage claim area and located our luggage. Thankfully McCall's provided a limo service to take us to the hotel so we didn't have to take a taxi. The limo ride was fascinating as well as enlightening. We were not accustomed to being pampered like this, and we agreed it was much better than riding as a passenger with our husbands at the wheel. The limo driver was far more courteous and responsive. Compared to Florence, traffic in NYC was horrendous. It didn't take long to figure out that taxi drivers ruled in the Big Apple. Jokingly, Anita compared it to being in the Indianapolis 500 race without a crash helmet. Thank goodness our limo driver was much more cautious than the taxi drivers.

We observed several close calls as pedestrians stepped off the curb intending to cross the street, and we closed our eyes each time. I visualized a taxi driver hitting a pedestrian and what a memory of our trip that would be. I made a comment about the taxi drivers being so reckless going through an intersection, and Anita remarked that perhaps traffic lights in NYC were just a suggestion. Unanimously, we decided if we did any walking on this trip, it was in our best interest to follow our mom's instruction to "Look both ways before crossing the street." Perhaps more practical than mom's admonition was to "Use extreme caution" when crossing the street."

When we arrived at the hotel, we were delighted that the trip was without an accident and that we were all in one piece. I think we individually said a "Thank you Lord for a good driver" prayer under our breath.

The Washington Jefferson Hotel is a beautiful old structure in Midtown NYC conveniently located to several prominent landmarks such as Times Square, Central Park, and Rockefeller Center. We checked in and went directly to our room and were more than pleased with our accommodations. Our meeting was scheduled for 10 a.m. that morning, so there was no time to spare. We unpacked, dressed and headed out for our meeting.

The limo was waiting for us and we were on our way to the McCall Company headquarters at 230 Park Avenue. The sights and sounds of downtown Manhattan were amazing. The streets were filled with automobiles and busses, traffic jams, honking horns of impatient drivers, and bicycle messengers in their bright colored shirts darting between the cars to deliver their messages on time. Multitudes of people scurried to and from their work locations.

Uncertain of the time required to get from the hotel to the McCall building because of the traffic, we arrived fifteen minutes in advance of our 10 a.m. appointment. The receptionist phoned a McCall's Corporate Administrative Assistant (AA) who promptly came out to meet us.

"Good morning Mrs. Johnson." said the AA. "You are a little early, but that is OK, better to be early than late."

"I hope that is not an inconvenience" I replied.

"Oh no, not at all. Travel time can be very unpredictable even for those of us living here. Let me show you to the conference room and let Mr. Hermann know you ladies are here. You will be comfortable, and coffee is available on the buffet table, if you would like some." Once we were in the room, the AA left and closed the door.

The impressive corporate conference room was like none I had ever seen. The large mahogany table had several high back leather chairs and a black blotter on the table at each chair. Hanging on the walls were impressively framed prints of McCall designer's fashion clothing. All were as beautiful as their photo on the pattern covers. On a table at one end of the room, several types of beautiful fabric, lace and trims were displayed. In my unrestrained and fanciful imagination, I could almost visualize the important business meetings, executive decisions, and deals made in this room. The ambiance of corporate sophistication was very evident everywhere I looked.

A silver coffee urn sat on the buffet table along with gold rimmed white china cups and saucers, real cream in the creamer and sugar squares in a bowl. Gold spoons lay neatly in a row next to the cups. Yumm, the aroma of fresh coffee tantalized my taste buds and after our busy morning, I was ready for coffee. I filled a cup and walked to the massive row of windows to have my first view of NYC.

The sky was remarkably clear that Tuesday. The sun was shining bright; the sky was a pale blue with a few small clouds floating by, and there was very little smog. Given what I had been told about the smog, I thought this was unusual. In the distance I could see several planes waiting to land at JFK where we arrived a short time before. As I stood looking out the window on the twenty-fourth floor, I could see the beautiful skyline of the city, the Hudson River and Central Park where the trees were just beginning to glow with the rich September fall colors of red and gold. It was truly a fascinating sight for this Alabama girl.

I was so engrossed in looking at the skyline and sights, I completely lost track of time. It startled me when the conference room doors opened and Mr. Hermann entered. He brought with him the ten dress samples we provided at the Atlanta Fabric Show.

"Good morning and welcome to New York," Mr. Hermann said. "I trust your flight was pleasant and the Washington Jefferson Hotel is to your liking."

"Yes, we had a great flight, and the hotel is absolutely fabulous. Thank you for arranging all this for us," I replied. "You have made us feel quite welcome already, and we are honored to be here.

Mr. Hermann poured himself a cup of coffee and we all took a seat around the conference table. We talked for about an hour and half recounting our backgrounds, sewing experience, discussing several of the sample dresses, and answering his questions. He was very polite but direct in his questions. Despite this politeness there was a little uncertainty in the air for us, which in retrospect, we should have anticipated. We came from a small fabric shop, had never been involved in the fashion design business at this level, and learned it was not a common practice for Mr. Hermann to use outside designers. McCall's employed a significant number of in-house, world-class designers, as we discovered later that afternoon. However, as the conversation continued, we grew more comfortable with Mr. Hermann as he did with us.

"Are you ladies ready for lunch?" Mr. Hermann asked after a while.

With no opportunity for breakfast that morning, we were famished to say the least. Not wanting to appear over anxious, I replied, "Yes, lunch would be nice."

"I know a little sandwich shop down the street, which is close by," Mr. Hermann said. "The food is good and most important, the service is fast. We have dinner reservations tonight at a great Italian restaurant, and I know you will enjoy that immensely. But for now, a quick sandwich will keep us on schedule." We spent the lunch hour enjoying our sandwiches, chips and soft drinks, exchanging personal and family information and becoming better acquainted.

CHAPTER 8

Meeting With The McCall's Design Committee

Never Let Someone Change Who You
Are to Become What They Need

AFTER LUNCH WE RETURNED TO McCall's office building and reconvened in the conference room. A short time after we arrived, the conference room doors opened and several people entered the room. We later learned this group consisted of McCall department managers, senior fashion designers and chief seamstresses.

Mr. Hermann had our ten sample dresses displayed for everyone to view. At that time, our design portfolio was limited to these ten sample dresses, and they were an integral component in convincing the McCall people we knew how to design and had long term design potential. This was our chance to market ourselves and our work, highlight our skills and showcase our creativity. It was important to demonstrate we took our design work seriously.

Anita and I stayed close to the dress samples answering a plethora of questions about our layout and design process, how we got our inspiration, the complexity of the pattern, of how many parts the pattern consisted, and the ease of use. The samples received detailed examinations by committee members resulting in mixed opinions. Some members commented on how adorable they were, while others- more skeptical -asked, "Do children really wear this type clothes?" I assumed those who thought the designs adorable had children and those asking the question did not. Overall, we were encouraged by the questions and tried to remain objective despite some members' perceived reluctance. We knew our positive attitude would be needed to close this deal and secure our contract.

After the initial dress inspection was complete, each representative filled a coffee cup and took a place at the conference table. One by one they introduced themselves and told us about their position in the company and their responsibilities. That was a lot to remember and I whispered to Anita, "I hope we are not tested on remembering names and titles." She chuckled and replied, "Me too."

Because McCall primarily produced patterns for women's and men's clothing, several representatives were unaware of the need for patterns for children's clothing. Therefore, we had a lot to talk about and some persuasion was required to secure a unanimous agreement.

Our preliminary discussions were intense with topics ranging from our backgrounds and concept design, to the frequency of pattern submissions to the technical and legal copyright issues. Based on the flow of the conversation, I thought it was apparent they were inclined to work with us, and we certainly wanted to be a part of the McCall's organization.

Around mid- afternoon, with no more questions to be asked and no more information requested from us, Mr. Hermann suggested we call it a day. We were bone tired and the committee needed time to contemplate this opportunity and decide whether or not it was in the best interest of the company to enter into a contract arrangement with outside designers.

Mr. Hermann reminded us of the dinner arrangements with him and several key members of the committee, and we were chauffeured back to the hotel. It was about 3:30 p.m. when we arrived at the Washington Jefferson and went to our room. We took off our shoes, secured a soft drink from the room convenience bar, and settled back into the comfortable chairs.

"Wasn't that fantastic?" I asked.

"It was," said Gail, "and I am so pleased with the way things went for us."

"We talked for a while longer then showered and dressed for dinner. I volunteered to be last, which gave me a bit more time for a quick nap, which I desperately needed.

The dinner reservation was for a delightful Italian restaurant and the cuisine was fantastic. I think we had pasta or ravioli, I'm not sure, but I remember the salad was wonderful and the desert was truly fantastic. We have some pretty good Italian restaurants in the Shoals area, but this was the best Italian food I had ever eaten. Our conversation never waned during dinner, and by the conclusion, I felt like we had made many more friends at McCall than just Mr. Hermann."

Toward the end of the meal, Mr. Hermann said, "We would like to treat you to a Broadway show tonight, if you are up to it."

Despite our weariness from a very long day, we were not going to pass up this opportunity. Our exposure to a Broadway type show was limited to our children's or grandchildren's school play or an occasional University of North Alabama theatrical production, so this would be delightful.

"We certainly are up to it, and thank you for your hospitality," I said.

We enjoyed the show immensely. But now, for the life of me, I can't remember the name of it. The limo dropped us off at the hotel, and we agreed we would continue our discussions the following morning at 9 a.m.

Mr. Hermann needed time to discuss the contract with his committee members and work out any lingering member reservations, so 9 a.m. was good in our opinion.

We were about dead when we opened the door to the room, I mean totally exhausted! We didn't tarry long before going to bed, and no one would have to rock us to sleep.

I had so many thoughts racing through my mind; I couldn't go to sleep despite being tired. Anita and Gail were already fast asleep, so I decided to make myself a cup of tea to see if that would help. As I sipped the tea I ventured to the window. Standing there looking out at all the bright lights, I could see what the night life was like in NYC. The streets and sidewalks were almost as busy as during the day. There were lights of all colors and sizes, some flashing while others turned periodically on a frame. I was amazed at the sight.

I thought to myself, we are in one of the most prominent and famous fashion design cities in the world. Even though high-fashion was not a significant part of the culture in Florence, I am well aware that Paris, New York, Milan, London, Barcelona and Rome have always had a major influence on fashion trends. A stroll down 5th Avenue in New York with its prestigious boutiques such as Versace, Chanel, Dior, and mainstream retailers such as Nike Town and Banana Republic had only been a fascination and dream for me, and yet here I was ready to take that stroll. Not as a visitor, but a fashion designer waiting to hopefully sign a contract with the McCall Pattern Company, one of the most recognized pattern companies in the world.

McCall is a privately owned international company established in 1870 by Scottish immigrant James McCall. They manufacture and sell patterns under the brand names of Butterick, McCall's and Vogue. For anyone involved in sewing, these pattern brand names and the prestige behind them were well known.

"How on earth did this Southern girl from Florence, Alabama get this opportunity?" I thought. I pinched myself to ensure it was real, and it was. After all my work and effort, here I was waiting to see if the McCall Pattern Company was interested in me as a children's clothing fashion designer. Pinch me again.

The tea did the trick, and after one cup I was relaxed and ready to go to sleep. My last thought before drifting off was simply, "I can't believe all that has happened today." In my nightly prayer I said, "Thank you God for giving us this opportunity, and whatever happens tomorrow, I know you will make it in our best interest."

CHAPTER 9

We Achieved Success

Today is a great day to be a great day

OUR WAKE UP CALL WEDNESDAY MORNING started our day at
6 a.m. Only ten minutes after we went to sleep, or so it seemed. Eager for
the activities to begin, we were out of bed without any encouragement. We
ordered bagels, cream cheese, fruit, and coffee from room service, a far cry
from the fried eggs, bacon, grits, biscuits and coffee we enjoyed at home, but
perhaps a bit healthier.

"Hey, I think we are getting the hang of this NYC lifestyle," I said to the
others. "If you have never had a New York bagel, you have missed something
wonderfully delicious."

We ate breakfast in the room, in between taking showers, drying hair,
putting on makeup and getting dressed. As you can imagine, three women
and one bathroom presented its challenges. Eventually, we were finally ready
to get this day started.

The limo was waiting at 8:40 a.m. to take us back to McCall's for our 9
a.m. meeting. We talked very little during the ride. I think we were all excited
and apprehensive simultaneously. This morning's meeting would be the cul-
mination of all our work efforts, aspirations and expectations. I said another
quick prayer as we exited the limo and went inside the building.

The same AA met us at the receptionist's desk and ushered us back into
the same conference room we were in the day before. We poured cups of coffee from the buffet table and waited anxiously for our meeting to begin. Soon

thereafter members of the committee entered the room with friendly morning greetings, inquired about our dinner and if we enjoyed the Broadway show. The more conversations we engaged in, the more comfortable I became. I took this as a good omen and a sign of success. I smiled and winked at Anita, and she smiled and winked back.

Mr. Hermann was the last to arrive and seemed to be in a jolly mood. He went directly to the conference table and took his seat. After some re-counting about the previous night's activities, a few business formalities and general conversation between members, he congratulated us and advised that the committee had decided to purchase three of the ten dress patterns immediately.

Needless to say Anita and I were elated. We could hardly contain our excitement. We both wanted to hug each other and shout for joy, but realized we needed to restrain ourselves and maintain our composure, so we nudged each other and smiled.

"As you are aware, we do not normally accept outside design work," Mr. Hermann said "but your style portrays a southern flare that is missing from our children's pattern portfolio, and I am not convinced that our in-house designers can replicate your design flare. So, we think these three patterns will be a good start for the spring line-up and we will see how they sell."

We continued our discussions, came to an agreement that if sales were good on these three patterns, the committee would consider a design contract with us.

After our discussion was completed, we toured the design room, pattern grading process, the fabric library, and a got firsthand demonstration of the interworking of a pattern company. It is truly an amazing process. By 10:45 a.m. we had completed our business and the tour. We said our good-byes, and the limo returned us to the hotel.

"I can't believe this," Anita said. "One of the biggest pattern companies in the world just bought three of our patterns, and may want to buy more. Can you believe this?"

"I can believe it," I said. "We did it! We did it! Now that it's over, let's celebrate our success. "What shall we do?" Anita asked.

Gail, contributing to the conversation, suggested we go sightseeing, the customary thing to do in NYC. After some discussion, sightseeing just did not hold our enthusiasm nor seem exciting, so Anita and I suggested going shopping. Although Gail reluctantly agreed, it was settled. Shopping it was.

Anita said, "I've always heard about New York's famous Garment District, so let's go there first."

"Sounds wonderful to me," I replied.

CHAPTER 10

Our Afternoon In New York

The Calm after the Storm

OUR RETURN FLIGHT TO HUNTSVILLE was Thursday morning at 10 a.m., so we had the entire afternoon free. We changed into casual clothing and headed out for the true NYC experience.

The first order of business was lunch. After considering several options, we decided that a New York hot dog from a street vendor would be not only an experience, but quick, and not impact our remaining shopping time. Several street vendors were available for our selection, and some looked more acceptable than others. Although Sabrett's claims the title "official sidewalk hot dog" in NYC, we selected a vendor who advertised wieners from the legendary Bronx sausage- maker, Stahl-Meyer. Now, that's about as authentic as you can get in NYC.

"A New York dog with everything and red onion relish" the vendor said as he handed me what looked like a complete meal on a bun. I gave it a once over thinking to myself, "What am I doing?"

"I hope whatever is on this hot dog will settle easy on my stomach" I said to Anita and Gail, and as I remember, it was delicious with no side affect on me. It was certainly different from the hot dogs I make at home, or any hotdog you would find in the South. It was fantastic.

With all the fascinating sights and historical landmarks available the obvious thing to do was locate a tour bus and take a ride around town as Gail had suggested. Not us. We were so focused on our purpose for being in NYC and our success that we spent the entire afternoon in the famous Garment District, in the heart of Midtown Manhattan. We went to Macy's, Lord & Taylor, Guess, and several specialty fabric, button, trim, and sewing-related shops. We were like children in a candy shop. We found so many beautiful fabrics we did not have in stock at Style Rite and we wanted to carry them home but knew we didn't have sufficient room in our luggage. We certainly fantasized how our dresses would look made of this high-end material.

The sidewalk was so crowded. People were everywhere, walking fast and bumping into each other frequently, intent on getting to their destination. It could be best described, in my opinion, as a mass of humanity. My only experience with this amount of human traffic was walking to Bryant-Denny stadium for a University of Alabama football game.

Most NYC people appeared to be in their own world, totally oblivious to anything or anyone around them. As they passed an apparent acquaintance, they often spoke loudly to each other and kept on walking. Much different from the streets of Florence where even if you were in a hurry, you exchanged greetings with a friendly stranger and stopped to talk to a friend or acquaintance for a minute before continuing on. That certainly was not the custom in NYC, but I guess there are too many people there to do that. Because the sidewalks were so crowded, we agreed to stay close together for fear of getting separated in the masses.

"Have you noticed how women dress?" Anita remarked. "I can't believe that here in one of the most famous fashion centers in the United States, some women dressed so, well, just tacky. I don't mean to be rude, but that's the only way I can describe it." We noticed how many women wore expensive business suits with, would you believe it, of all things, athletic shoes. I could not believe what I was seeing.

You see, in the South we would never do that. Athletic shoes were reserved for denim jeans, exercise wear, or a warm up suit. Wearing them with dress or business attire, is just not appropriate, and as Anita put it, just tacky. Only after walking in heels for several city blocks, trying to maintain our balance as people in the crowd bumped into us, and waiting on traffic lights, did we fully understand the rationale behind the unorthodox attire of NYC women. By the conclusion of our shopping, our legs were tired and our feet were aching. Knowing the benefits of that athletic shoe trick before we left the hotel would have been priceless. We decided that the Big Apple could teach us Southern gals a few things.

After a couple of hours shopping, we thought seriously about finding a sport's wear shop and purchasing athletic shoes, but decided against it. We had athletic shoes at home and didn't really need another pair. "Let's tough it out," Gail said, and Anita and I reluctantly agreed.

We found our way back to the hotel and crashed for an hour or so before going to dinner. Tired but delighted, I knew that afternoon in NYC would be remembered for my lifetime.

CHAPTER 11

The McCall - Ruffles and Lace Agreement

*Once in a Lifetime you find something
which changes Everything*

GENETT, ANITA AND GAIL RETURNED HOME to Florence, the Style Rite Fabrics Shop and their design work, but trying to keep their mind on the day-to-day business was difficult. The anticipation was so great, spring seemed such a long time away, and they had no choice but to wait. Genett said, "Knowing what happened to Job in the Bible story, I decided not to pray for patience, but to simply pray for endurance. My patience had already been tested as much as I wanted it to be."

Spring finally arrived and sure enough, the McCall pattern catalogue included the three Ruffles and Lace designs. "I cannot describe the exuberance and excitement we felt seeing our dress creations in the catalogue. This level of personal achievement was almost more than we could imagine" Genett stated.

The catalogue included my favorite design, a smartly tailored Sunday dress style, with white piping and accessorized with white French lace. However, the eye-catching design was a small checked red gingham dress with rows and rows of ruffles, a Peter Pan collar, puffed sleeves with ruffles, and a sash which tied in the back- a simply gorgeous little dress. Needless to say, we were overjoyed to see our Ruffles and Lace designs in the catalogue and so were our customers. We had made the big time.

As would be expected, McCall's wanted to see how popular our designs would be in this first catalogue before any further agreements or discussion. Anticipating a good response, we continued our design and dress making. Preparing for a dress design to be included in the catalogue requires advance work. In fact, McCall designers work almost a year in advance to get their patterns ready for publication, and as independent designers, we were no different.

Preparation for the catalogue publication schedule was a little more complex than we were accustomed to, because previously, we made the pattern and dress at our leisure and in sufficient time for the upcoming season. We realized all too well that arrangement would be changed if we were fortunate enough to get an agreement.

The sales of our patterns exceeded McCall's expectations and they wanted more designs. Mr. Hermann phoned in the fall and wanted to discuss a formal agreement. This time I went to NYC alone to discuss terms and conditions about our ability to provide patterns and the time frame to meet McCall's expectations. We met in the same impressive conference room with Mr. Hermann and several of the same people Anita and I met in our previous session. Our discussions were significantly different this time, and I felt more comfortable and at ease. I was welcomed so well, I felt part of the McCall team before our meeting began.

On our first trip, I remembered thinking about the important business deals made in this conference room, and now here I am ready to discuss our deal with McCall's. I poured coffee from the same silver coffee urn into the same beautiful gold rimmed white china cups, and used one of the gold spoons which lay neatly in a row next to the cups. Once again I took a couple of minutes to gaze out the window at the NYC skyline before taking my seat at the conference table. It was fall again and my memory quickly recalled how excited and uncertain life was the last time I looked out this window. Things had changed and I felt good about this meeting.

"Welcome back to New York City, and congratulations on your designs being received so well" said Mr. Hermann. "We had no idea how your Southern style would be received, and much to our surprise, it has gone over very well. I think we can help each other in a big way. You will have a venue to make your designs available to a much broader group, and we can offer a variety of children's clothing patterns we have not been able to do previously. Looks like a win-win to me."

I thought to myself, "Yes sir, and you have no idea how big this win is for us."

"We are also surprised, and delighted, at how well the sales have been" I said. "We knew they were pretty dresses, and we hoped other women would think so."

"Evidently they did and I am amazed at the interest these dresses have created in all of our markets," said McCall's chief design manager as she gave her congratulations. "Sales are strong across all sections of the United States and we have received several orders from outside the United States. So you are internationally recognized from the beginning. It's like a new design concept for children, and we have missed it all these years. Thank goodness you are here. I can hardly wait to get you on the regular catalogue schedule."

Mr. Hermann launched into the legal and technical aspects of an agreement, and we discussed, questioned, and debated each one to my understanding. One of the agreement stipulations was our personal names could not be used in any promotion or advertisement of the patterns.

"We will however, recognize a design business name when you create one," Mr. Hermann stated.

"We have already selected a business name, and developed and registered a trademark." I said.

Mr. Hermann seemed somewhat astonished at our efficiency and proactive action. "Very good" he said nodding his head affirmatively.

Realizing the possibilities after our first trip to McCall's, Anita and I had consulted with an attorney prior to this NYC trip to discuss what we needed in the event we secured an agreement. The attorney suggested we create a business name and file a trademark for it.

Neither Anita nor I had created a business for ourselves, so choosing a name was a challenge. We thought about several options without consensus on any of them. We wanted to keep the name simple but easy recognizable.

We were sitting at the cutting table brainstorming and looking at the dresses we had made, and I remarked, "When you look at this dress, what first catches your eye?"

"The lace and ruffles," Anita responded.

"Me, too," I said, "so, since the McCall's design staff greatly admired our southern dress concept, and we will be incorporating lots of lace and several ruffles in our designs, what do you think about Ruffles and Lace for our name?"

Anita said, "It has a good sound to it, I like it."

After additional discussions, we decided that Ruffles and Lace was a good descriptive business name. We developed the Ruffles and Lace signature name design originally used on the McCall patterns and later modernized it integrating 'treasured collection' into the name.

Once we agreed on our business name, we thought we should also have a logo or design to define us. Something eye catching, cute, and representative of our design style. We shared ideas for several days and finally agreed the logo should be a little girl in a dress with ruffles and lace. Anita's aunt, Mrs. Norma Fisher, was a sketch artist and created the logo below, which was included in our trademark registration.

With the assistance of our attorney, Anita and I developed a partnership agreement at the same time as the name and trademark, and we were ready to conduct business with McCall's. Ruffles and Lace was a living entity and soon to be a household word with all sewing enthusiasts.

Mr. Hermann continued his discussion presenting the financial arrangements for the purchase of our dresses and royalties from pattern sales. I thought they were equitable, and agreed in principal with the terms of the agreement, subject to our attorneys review. We concluded our business discussions and I returned to the hotel waiting my four a.m. red eye flight home the following day.

I phoned Anita from the hotel to let her know about the meeting results and the agreement. "I can hardly believe it has happened," Anita said. "In my wildest imagination I never dreamed that one day we would be working side-by-side with professional designers in the largest pattern company in the United States."

"Me either" I said. "It has been a long road since I sat at Mama's feet pushing that old treadle machine, learning how to sew my dresses. I have come a long way since then. See you tomorrow"

I had little trouble falling asleep that night and returned home exuberated and excited.

When I arrived at the shop the following day, a group of loyal patrons met me with coffee and doughnuts in celebration of our success. We ordered a good number of patterns from our first three dresses in the catalogue and sold every one the day they arrived. Customers were asking us to autograph their patterns and we felt like real celebrities. A copy of three of our early patterns in the 1983 and1984 McCall's catalogue is included on the following pages.

We continued to sell our Style Rite Fabrics merchandise and make and display dresses for the shop. Business was good and we were happy. A few months after the agreement with McCall's, Gail's husband was transferred to another state by his company. Because she was physically unable to be present at our work design sessions, she said farewell to our business venture and wished us continued success. Although Gail was not part of our formal partnership, she was an early design contributor, and we appreciated her input.

Needless to say designing dresses for McCall's kept Anita and I quite busy the next few years. We always had several designs in the works, changing them frequently as ideas came to us. As an extra bonus to entice McCall pattern sales, we added a doll feature to the dress pattern. After the dress making process was completed, we reduced the pattern to doll size and made a dress exactly like the child's dress. We cut out a cloth doll, sewed it together, stuffed it with cotton and dressed it to match. We included the doll dress pattern along with the regular pattern, so the young lady could have a doll dressed the same as her. That was well received and Anita and I did that for several years. In time, moms lost interest in the doll dress feature, and we subsequently discontinued providing it with the dress pattern.

This is one of our early patterns published in
the 1983 McCall Pattern Catalogue.

This darling little dress is a cotton print with a contrasting print or solid
front bodice and optional skirt ruffle. It has a Peter Pan collar with an accent
ribbon, puff or long sleeves, and a sash, which ties in the back.

This pattern was published in the 1984 McCall Pattern Catalogue.

This cute dress is a cotton print with pin tucks on the front bodice. It has a rounded collar with gathered lace and optional long, short, or three-quarter sleeves. The accent waist ribbon tie sash puts the finishing touch on this ensemble.

This is another of our patterns published in the
1984 McCall Pattern Catalogue.

This Sunday dress is classy in either a print or solid with the bordered eyelet overlay, Peter Pan collar, and optional long or short sleeves. The contrasting solid or ribbon cummerbund or a wide ribbon sash completes this elegant look.

Conclusion of Style Rite Fabrics

You Will Never Know Just How Important
You Have Been To Me.

I CONTINUED TO OPERATE STYLE RITE FABRICS until 1990 when a long time customer, Ellen Smith and her husband Jimmy, approached me about buying the shop. Ellen had desired to own a fabric shop for many years but the right opportunity never seemed to come along. Because she knew how well Style Rite Fabrics operated and the loyal customer base Anita and I had developed, she asked if I would be interested in selling. I had no desire to sell at that time, so I initially declined her offer. Ellen was persistent and asked me again a few months later to give her a sales price. Although I had given no consideration to selling immediately, I did realize that selling would be inevitable in the years ahead. I had to do some real soul searching about selling my shop.

Style Rite Fabrics had become very successful and a significant part of me and my daily activities. If you own or manage a business, you know how much time it takes away from your family and personal life. The retail business can be ruthless and requires total dedication if you are to be profitable. It doesn't care that you have a sick child, or if your spouse insists you make plans for a vacation, or if your automobile breaks down and you have to take it to the repair shop. The truth is, if you are not attending to business, you lose. Retail has no mercy. Therefore, often I felt married to the shop more than to my husband, and although Bill never complained, I am certain he felt the same way.

It was not unusual for me to put in sixty plus hours a week in addition to fulfilling my responsibilities as a wife and mother plus my church activities. It really takes some managing to keep that many people happy, and I think I learned how to do that sufficiently with a lot of help from Bill and my children.

Around this time, as president of the Florence Business Women's Club, I was scheduled to attend a convention in Orlando, Florida, so Bill and I decided to drive down. The drive time would give us ample opportunity to discuss Ellen's offer and decide what we should do. I say what 'we' should do, but in reality it was my shop and I knew Bill would support me in whatever decision I made. However, I wanted him to be part of that decision.

"Are you ready to sell?" Bill asked.

"I am not sure. I haven't thought much about it," I said.

"Do you think you will want to sell in the next couple of years?" he asked.

"I probably will," I replied. "but, by that time, I will have prepared myself to sell."

"What if there is no buyer at that time?" Bill said. "What will you do then?"

What a sobering thought. What if no one is interested? What if the economy is slow and money is tight? What if sales slump and the shop is not saleable? By that time, the lease will be up for renewal, and what if it is not renewed? I pondered all these questions as we drove.

I had a thousand questions and scenarios running through my mind. I sat quietly for several miles watching the beautiful scenery considering the how to's and what if's for every scenario I could imagine.

Bill and I took time to speculate on the sale option periodically throughout the next two days as I attended the conference, and we played a couple rounds of golf, and enjoyed some delicious fresh seafood coastal dining. Finally we agreed that if I planned to sell within the next two years, now was the opportune time to make Ellen an offer. When we returned to Florence, I contacted Ellen and made her an offer that she and Jimmy accepted immediately.

After sixteen years owning Style Rite Fabrics, time had come to say good-bye to something that had been a vital part of my life. Something which had given me confidence to stand up for myself, helped me to develop into an astute business woman, reinforced my belief in the Golden Rule, helped me make many new friends, taught my daughter the fundamentals of customer relationships, provided a part-time job for several ladies, and created so many long-lasting memories. It was like saying good-by to an old friend. The transfer documents were prepared and signed drawing to a conclusion my ownership of Style Rite Fabrics. I volunteered to stay on for a while as Ellen made the transition and became more comfortable in her new role as owner and eventually she no longer needed me.

THROUGH THE YEARS
Growing up

Genett age 3

Genett age 5

Coffee High School 1952

Coffee High School 2015

THROUGH THE YEARS
At McCalls Pattern Company

Genett and Carolyne Cafaro at McCall's Pattern Company

McCall's Design Room

Genett at the published pattern board in her home sewing room

THROUGH THE YEARS
The Susan G Komen Foundation Golf Tournament

Ambassador Genett giving instructions at the "Rally For A Cure" golf tournament.

2015 Tournament Participants

Genett receiving a Phil Mickelson autographed "Rally For A Cure" flag

CHAPTER 13

Continuation of Ruffles and Lace

What I Love Most About My Business
are Those I Share it With.

THE END OF STYLE RITE FABRICS did not signal the end of our design work- far from it. Without the daily management requirements of Style Rite Fabrics, I had an excess of time which could be devoted to working on new designs. That said however, I never anticipated the withdrawal problems I experienced after the sale. Because I never stopped to consider how much of my time Style Rite Fabrics demanded, all at once I had lots of time but not enough activities to fill it, even with our continued design work. I wanted to find activities to fill that additional available time.

A local department store, Pizitz, advertized for part-time jobs over the Christmas season and I applied. My background in children's clothing fit very nicely with their opening in the children's department, so they hired me. That part-time job helped to fill the void for a few months. At least my schedule was temporarily full again. Unfortunately, when that job was over, I was back to square one.

I satisfied part of my time reading and cooking, two things I enjoyed but I didn't get an opportunity to do much of as a shop owner. My fabric shop competitors, Mike and Ceda Hambrick realized my dilemma and suggested I teach a sewing class for their customers, which I eagerly agreed to do. That was a lot of fun, but it didn't involve much time each week, and I desperately needed something else in which to be involved.

Three of my close friends and I lunched occasionally and during a lunch one friend complained that her husband spent far more time playing golf than she liked, but she did not know what to do about it. Well, being the good friends we were, we felt it incumbent to find a solution to our friend's problem. After discussing several options, we decided what was good for the goose should be good for the gander, and our decision was to learn to play golf. That sounded like a good solution and an interesting activity. We could play a round of golf and then have lunch together as often as we wanted. Additionally from my perspective, golfing was something I could do as frequently as I desired on an individual basis, and since Bill also played, a twosome should work out fine. It would also provide good exercise as well. I enjoyed our golf lessons very much and started playing several times a week. Golf grew to be as much a passion for me as Style Rite Fabrics previously did and that passion continues today.

For the past fourteen years, I have had the opportunity to work as an Ambassador for the annual Susan G. Komen Foundation "Rally for the Cure" golf tournament held at the Blackberry Trail Golf Course in Florence. This aggrandized tri-state event includes the states of Alabama, Mississippi and Tennessee. It is one of the largest ladies' tournaments in the Southeast drawing a hundred plus participants at each year. During my fourteen year involvement, the tournament has raised some $88,000 to contribute to breast cancer awareness programs.

Between my golf outings, Anita and I continued to design. I set up my basement as a functional design space several years before selling Style Rite Fabrics, so Anita and I continued to have our morning coffee there as we sketched and created new designs. The basement included an adequate amount of space needed to work comfortably. It provided a large cutting board area, good lighting, storage and primary and secondary work centers so we could each have our own space.

Creating new designs is always a challenge and we are frequently asked where we get our ideas. Well, as most artists, a new idea is an inspiration which can come from anything anywhere, at anytime. We are open to any idea that can translate to children's clothing. Fortunately our thought process is more alike than different. We play off each other's ideas adding, revising, modifying, and deleting until an idea has a formulation. We never discount any idea until we explore it thoroughly. Sometimes it comes to fruition and a pattern is created, and there are times an idea is totally scuttled.

Our concept of Ruffles and Lace was to create children's clothing which is simple, functional and consistent. In our opinion, one pattern should encompass more than a single year's usage, and should be adaptable for several garment variations with just a few simple changes, creating a new and different look. "While hemline length and ruffle width have fluctuated through the years, the basic idea behind Ruffles and Lace hasn't. We are not faddish or high fashion," Genett said in a *Times Daily* newspaper interview. "We have a cute, sweet look that's always stylish and isn't in one minute and gone the next." We believe and still do, that is the type pattern moms want to use.

Often when Anita and I go on a trip together, such as the Atlanta fabric market, and are in the car for several hours, we can become quite creative, taking an idea and building on it step by step. We always carry sketch pads with us and it is not unusual to have a pretty good design by the time we arrive at our destination. If we don't, it has still been a profitable discussion to put on paper; we may find a way to incorporate the idea into another pattern later on.

"Sleepless nights are also a haven for creativity." Genett says, "If I can't sleep, I get up and rough sketch designs. It is amazing how alert and creative the brain can be at three o'clock in the morning. It is also a good way to make myself tired. By the time my brain has been adequately taxed, my mind and eyes, are tired and sleep is a good reward for designing another outfit I will discuss with Anita later that day."

Designing is both a joy and a labor. McCall's expects us to submit to their chief designer at least four designs per season to review for each catalogue. Originally McCall's had four seasons per year, so creating and designing sixteen outfits kept us busy all year. We usually have one or two designs accepted from each submission. In March 2016, we submitted four designs and McCall's accepted three of them within three days after receipt. Our work is still in demand. Two of our patterns in the 2016 catalogue are included on the following pages.

After thirty-four years together designing children's clothing, the excitement has waned a bit. Anita and I work more independently now, meeting on a sporadic basis to share ideas or critique our designs. Our fingers are not as nimble and our eyesight has diminished a little requiring more use of the dreaded seam ripper than it used to. We still meet McCall's submission each season, although it gets more difficult, and I suspect that our design work will come to a conclusion in a few years. However, I don't think I will experience the same withdrawal problems when we close Ruffles and Lace as I did with Style Rite Fabrics, and we will be ready to move on to our next life experiences.

Since we made the agreement with McCall's in 1982, we have submitted approximately 300 designs to McCall's, of which they have purchased some 225. These purchases, which were included in McCall's season catalogues, translate to some 1,250,580 patterns sold. Not bad for two hometown ladies from Florence, Alabama, huh?

This pattern was published in the 2016 McCall Pattern Catalogue.

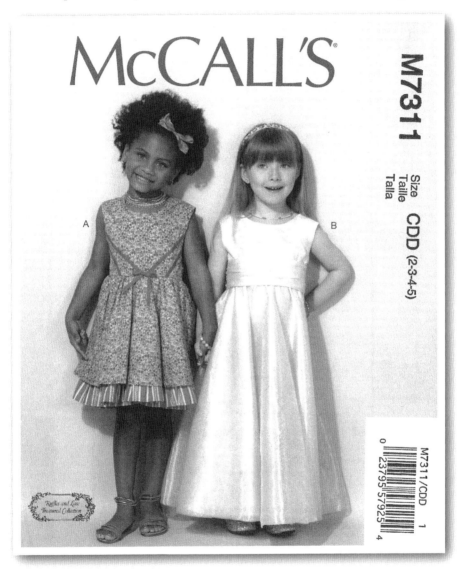

This versatile pattern includes a standard bodice with a "V"ed back. It has a gathered skirt, no collar and can be made with sleeves or sleeveless. There is an option for an underskirt with a contrasting ruffle creating a playful look. The matching cummerbund provides a more formal look.

This pattern was also published in the 2016 McCall Pattern Catalogue.

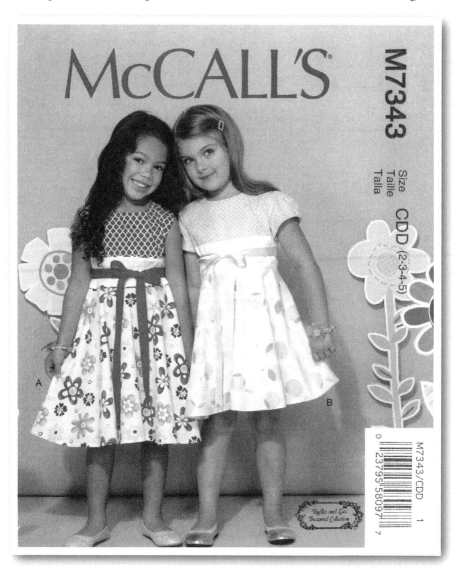

This springtime dress features a high bodice with a midriff, a circle skirt and a sewn in cummerbund accented with a wide ribbon. It can be made with sleeves or sleeveless.

CHAPTER 14

My Sewing Inspirations

Some of the greatest blessings in my life call me G.G.

CREATIVE INSPIRATIONS COME FROM MANY different sources in many different ways Genett says. For many years, my daughter Debbie was my only inspiration. She was patient enough to spend many hours with me as I cut, sewed, adjusted and redesigned a dress until it had the look I wanted. For the past few years my great-granddaughters, Olivia and Layla, have been a significant part of my inspiration. They are such beautiful little girls with such vivid imitations; they inspire my imagination, and have unknowingly been the source of many of my design creations. When I develop a design concept, **I** imagine how the outfit will look on one of them. They are always so appreciative of the dresses I make for them, and never hesitate to ask about their next dress.

"One day Olivia, my oldest great granddaughter, came into the sewing room when I was making a sample dress for one of our patterns.

"Is that dress for me?" Olivia asked excitingly.

"No, I will send it to the pattern company," I replied, "but I'm going to make you more dresses, not like this one because we don't want anyone to have a dress like yours."

Knowing she would have more dresses made Olivia happy. She said, "OK," and with doll in hand skipped out of the room. This is a photo of Olivia wearing one of our Ruffles and Lace designs.

Genett states, "I have always taken pride in my sewing whether I was making a simple play outfit or a sophisticated antebellum style dress with ruffles and lace. Mama always told me, 'If you take time to make it right, it will last a long time.' She was right, as usual."

Debbie validates that statement with this amazing story. "When our oldest granddaughter, Jenni, was nine months old Mother made her an heirloom, 'hand-sewn' dress, slip, and bonnet for her nine month panel picture. I believe this was the first hand-sewn dress Mother had ever made.

After Jenni outgrew it our daughter, Sondra, returned the dress and bonnet back to me, and I kept it until the next granddaughter, Emma, who is fifteen years old now, was nine months old, and she wore it to have her picture made. The dress came back to me again when she could no longer wear it. When Olivia, our seven year old granddaughter, was nine months old she, too, had her picture made wearing this dress.

A couple of years later, Layla, five years old now, came along and she continued the tradition and had her nine month panel picture made wearing this little dress. Jenni married that year and Layla wore the dress to Jenni's wedding -- such a special thing to see them together.

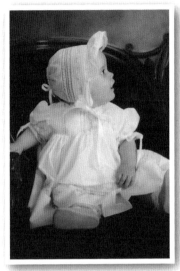

Jenni's photo in the hand-made dress

Layla wearing the hand-made dress with Jenni

Now, the dress and bonnet are back to the original owner, Jenni, who has just given birth to a little girl of her own, Faris, will be the fifth generation to wear this dress at nine months old. Mother never imagined that her first effort at 'hand-sewing' would be around and still being worn twenty- seven years later!"

Debbie also told of another memorable event involving another hand-sewn dress. "Layla loved the Easter dress G.G. made for her in 2016. Layla over-heard the adults talking about the dress when Mother said it would most likely be the last hand-sewn dress she would make, since her eyesight and arthritis has made hand sewing difficult. That comment really disturbed Layla and she went to Mother almost in tears, asking if G.G. would never make any more dresses for her. She thought she'd have to go without pretty dresses from now on. Mother assured her that she would still sew for her, but just wouldn't be hand-making anything. Needless to say, that sure made Layla much happier!" Here is Layla wearing Mother's last hand sewn dress.

CHAPTER 15

A Partner's Perspective

Anita Jaynes, Seamstress and Ruffles and Lace Partner
God gives us talents and we must uncover them for ourselves

I COME FROM A LONG LINE of ancestors whose gifted hands created beautiful things. There are wood craftsmen, artist, seamstresses, quilters, fine embroiders, and musicians in my family history. My grandfather taught my daddy not only the skill of building something from wood, but how to properly finish it as well. He encouraged quality building, which would last for a long time, and instilled the importance of creating something with which Daddy would be proud to have his name associated. Daddy earned the title of Master Carpenter as a result of the instruction and training he received. He passed his knowledge along to my two brothers who also became skilled craftsmen. My brothers received recognition from the state of Alabama for their work restoring and reproducing chairs in the senate chamber. Their restoration work can also be found in many historic homes in Alabama.

On my mother's side, artistry and creativity was also abundant. My aunt possessed the ability to sketch and paint, and she created some beautiful landscapes. She grew up during a time when art canvases were difficult to acquire, so she painted on anything available, and often that was a piece of discarded sheetrock. My grandmother made dresses for her five daughters and fashioned beautiful handmade quilts. One of my great aunts was extremely skilled in hand embroidery, a craft that has almost been lost today.

My talented mother made many dresses for me and my dolls, and that is when I was introduced to the art of sewing. I sat and watched my mother make dresses from the fabric she purchased in town. She always chose beautiful fabrics, and when she finished the dress was perfect. I loved all the things she made for me, and as most children, I had my favorites. As I sewed for my daughter, it was a gratifying feeling to apply some of the sewing techniques I had seen my mother use.

I first met Genett when I was as a customer of Style Rite Fabrics. I liked to shop there because it was a magical shop filled with bolts of fine fabrics and a 'mother lode' of sewing supplies. Bright colors and pattern mixing has always played a big part in selecting my fabrics. My appreciation for the natural beauty of God's color pallet is evident in everything I make. The varying shades of green leaves against a blue sky, soft white clouds, the turquoise blue of the ocean framed with pearly white sand, and bright green grass with golden yellow wildflowers and white buttercups, to describe just a few.

Part of my love for creating beautiful things is designing and sewing children's clothing. I would carefully choose just the right prints and trims, and was proud when I made something for my daughter. However, I was my most fierce critic. I often critiqued my finished product and saw things that were unsatisfactory to me. It looked too 'homemade' in my estimation, and I didn't like that. What made it look 'homemade', and why was I not happy with the way it looked? What could I do to make a difference in the design? What was the difference in my dress compared to the dress purchased in a department store? I continued with more determination than ever, and would make many changes before I could say, "I am proud to put my name on this dress." That is one of many sewing traits Genett and I share in common.

When I needed a part time job, Genett hired me to work at Style Rite Fabrics. I enjoyed working for her and she taught me many new sewing techniques. I also learned valuable work ethics from Genett, including the principle that all customers and their needs were top priority. We worked side by side and in

1981, we began to design our own dresses. We made sample dresses to display in the shop, and to our surprise, our customers wanted to make dresses just like ours.

Before we met with McCall's, we created our designs on a leisurely basis, but with their interest in our designs got serious. We were confident we could give sewing enthusiasts other options that would be more of a challenge than the mundane A-line dresses that seemed to be the trend in the children's section of the McCall's catalogue in the 1980s. Seeing our designs published in the McCall's catalogue had a significant impact on me. It gave me a sense of accomplishment and a drive to create more and better designs. I love what I do and Genett does also.

Do I feel lucky? I think blessed is a better word. I give God the glory for all I have been able to do. Hopefully Genett and I will have many more years of this amazing adventure we embarked on some thirty-five years ago. Working with Genett has taught me well.

My Favorite Pattern

No one else sees the world quite the way you do

EACH OF OUR 225 DESIGNS included in the McCall pattern catalogues is unique, pretty and delightful, and selecting one as "my favorite" is difficult. However, Debbie and I have selected two favorite patterns to share with you along with why they are our favorite.

Genett H. Johnson

This is a special pattern to me. It can be a sweet church dress made of a bordered white eyelet, with pastel ribbons and a jacket for church. Take the jacket off and it can be a party dress. If it is made in a bright, fun fabric it can be worn to school or Grandma's house. It can be made with ribbon, lace, or other trim. You can just have fun creating your own dress from your own ideas.

Debbie Johnson May

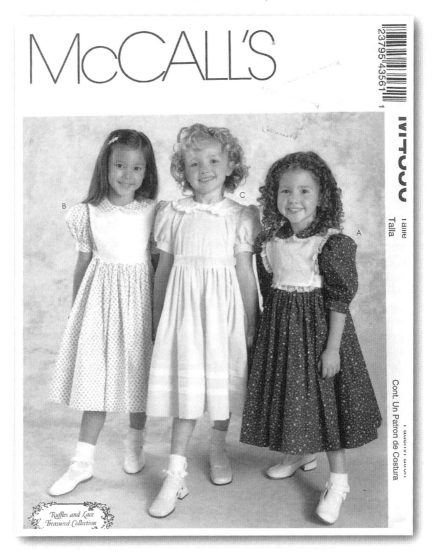

McCALL'S

I loved this little bib pinafore. It changed the entire dress and gave you a two-for-one deal. It is made in a pastel with a white bib that was so sweet for church or party wear. But, when it is made with a calico fabric and contrasting solid bib, it looked old-fashioned and almost prairie-like. I think this one is a classic and timeless look.

Impacts and Impressions

Your Best Friends Are Those Who Know
How Truly Loved They Are.

AS I THINK BACK OVER my life experiences I remember so many people who have made an impression or impact on my life. People who have been great friends, provided encouragement, advice, and moral support to me. Without these friends, I would not have made it through some difficult times. I love each one and treasure their friendship. I appreciate their willingness to submit comments for this book which we have included with their permission.

Carolyne Cafaro
McCall's Patterns
New York, New York

"For over thirty-two years Ruffles and Lace has provided The McCall Pattern Company with wonderful designs that appeal to the little girl in all of us. Creative and innovative, the designs have been fashionably current yet reflect the traditional looks that both mother and daughter love. It has been a pleasure to work with Genett and we are proud to have her as part of the McCall team."

Ceda Hambrick
Owner Fabric Finders, Inc.
Florence, Alabama

"Over the years, I have had a great friendship with Genett. As a customer as well as a teacher, she was always a great person to work with. We were proud to sell her patterns in our business and our customers and employees were always happy to see Genett and ask her opinion on their sewing projects. I am so happy for her and her accomplishments. She has a rare talent and uses it so often for the benefit of others. She is one of a kind!"

Mary Berry
Former part-time employee
Cypress Inn, Tennessee

"I met Genett when she bought the Style Rite Fabrics shop. As a matter of fact, I was one of her first customers. My husband and I live on a farm in Tennessee, and each week when he took a load of calves to the sale barn, I went with him. I would shop at Style Rite Fabrics while he was at the sale. During this time, I had three little girls and I sewed for them and myself frequently. I looked forward to seeing the latest fabric and newest McCall patterns, and I always returned home with plenty of material to sew. Genett's daughter Debbie was helpful in selecting my fabric and patterns, and Genett had thread, buttons and trim to make a beautiful garment. I left a happy customer every trip I made.

After the girls grew up, I found myself lonely and without much to do, so I went to work at Style Rite Fabrics on a part-time basis. I worked there until Genett sold the shop in 1990. I loved every minute we were together, and we have continued our friendship over these many years. My three daughters, who gave me beautiful grand children, have developed the same love for sewing as I did. The only thing is, they do not have a Style Rite Fabrics or a Genett to visit as I did. It was great to be with Genett and shop at her shop. I made many friends there."

Susan McCutcheon
Retired Northwest Shoals Community College Instructor
Florence, Alabama

"I met Genett soon after she bought her fabric shop while sewing for my daughter and myself. When my daughter became a teenager, she no longer wanted 'homemade clothes,' so Genett would give me imitation designer labels which I would sew into the clothes I made. My daughter thought the clothes were store bought and she was happy. A visit to the Style Rite Fabric shop and a conversation with Genett was always a therapy treatment for me. While balancing our check book one day, my husband made the remark that if we could ever get Style Rite Fabrics paid off, we would be in good shape. Genett and I have remained good friends for several years."

Doris Stutts
Retired Collinwood High School Teacher
Iron City, Tennessee

"The first time I met Genett she was in the process of buying Style Rite Fabric shop. We had a mutual interest immediately as we both liked sewing and fine fabrics. I taught Home Economics at Collinwood High School in Tennessee for several years, and as soon as school was out on Friday, my daughter and I would head to Style Rite Fabrics to shop. My daughter loved going there and we would buy what we needed to sew for the weekend and following week. Style Rite Fabrics was a one stop shop because Genett always had everything we needed for our sewing projects. My daughter developed a love for sewing and also learned how to smock and French hand- sew. McCall Patterns sponsored a teen sewing contest one year and Genett and I encouraged my daughter to enter. She made and entered two beautiful dresses and just as we expected, she won. She and I were given a trip to New York where she was presented a sewing machine as her prize. The editors of McCall magazine published an article about her sewing abilities and accomplishments, and needless to say Genett and I were very proud of her. Genett and I do not see each other very often, but when we do, we talk of all the fun we had together. Thanks to Genett for Style Rite Fabrics and all the help she gave to me and my daughter."

Revonda Twesme
Loyal Customer and Golf Friend
Florence, Alabama

"I moved to Florence in 1991 and soon after, met Genett at the Style Rite Fabric Shop. My mother was a wonderful and creative seamstress, so I had been around sewing all my life, but I never really learned how to sew. After talking with Genett, I realized that she sewed like my mother, knowing ways to make a garment look the best. Oh my goodness, this was the person to teach me. I would go to Genett's house where she taught me French hand sewing, smocking, and other sewing techniques. She encouraged me to call her with any type of sewing question, even after we ended our lessons. We continued a friendship through the years, and believe me, I called her frequently with sewing questions. After my children grew up and I began golfing, I was able to visit with Genett in her next role—at Blackberry Trail golf course. What a wonderful gift she shared with so many as she imparted her knowledge and a love for hand sewing. She also blessed me with a chance to feel closer to my mom."

Sandra Harper
Retired Lauderdale County Extension Agent
Florence, Alabama

"I first met Genett while I was a student in the University of North Alabama (UNA) Home Economics program. She was a frequent guest lecturer in our Clothing and Textiles classes. Our professor, Florine Rasch, advised us that Style Rite Fabric Shop was the best place in town to buy fabrics, so that's where I shopped for the fabric I used in my classes. After graduation, I found employment as a county extension agent and left Florence for four years. During that time however, I held fast to the lessons Genett taught me at UNA. As I worked as an agent, she became my bedrock and go to business woman for all my fabric needs and questions. Genett taught classes for several extension agencies in the area, judged garments for 4-H members on multiple levels, and assisted with our fashion shows. She was a wonderful friend to me and a great supporter of our programs. Her history with the extension service is such a vital part of the 'fabric of the life' of UNA students all over the country. We all benefited from her wealth of knowledge and the values she shared with us. Thank you Genett for sharing your history with me, and all those who know and treasure you."

In Appreciation

Trade your expectation for appreciation
and the world changes instantly

"*T*HERE ARE SO MANY PEOPLE who have been part of my life in such a prominent way. I wish to acknowledge and thank them for contributing to my fulfilled life, and their influence on the measure of success I have achieved. They encouraged me to face life's challenges, persevere through the difficult times, and shared the good times with me. I could not have done this without their support.

I extend my sincere appreciation to all my business associates because your involvement in Style Rite Fabrics Shop and Ruffles and Lace made my story much more interesting.

Thanks to all my loyal customers who helped make Style Rite Fabrics a profitable investment and a fun place to work for sixteen years.

I express my gratefulness to the McCall Pattern Company for providing me the opportunity to expand my business of children's clothing design and live out my dream.

I am thankful to my nephew Charles for suggesting that we write this book, his diligence in helping me remember old information, and creating the opportunity to rekindle some lost friendships. His recommendations and suggestions have made my story come alive through this book.

And last but not least, thanks to all my friends. Without you, to whom would I tell my story?"

Recognition and Accomplishments

*Behind every great accomplishment, there
is an even greater opportunity.*

IN ADDITION TO THE PERSONAL SATISFACTION of being successful as a business woman, entrepreneur, fashion designer, and accomplished
seamstress, Genett has also received recognition though her participation in,
and support of, the organizations listed below.

President, Florence Business Women's Club

Secretary, North Florence Business Association

Honorary Member of the Lauderdale County 4-H Club

Guest Lecturer, University of North Alabama
Department of Human Environmental Sciences and Merchandising

Guest Instructor, University of Alabama's Department of Apparel and Textiles

Guest Teacher, Bradshaw High School Home Economic Class

Facilitator, Specialized Sewing Classes for Hambrick Fabric Shop

Ambassador, Susan G. Komen Foundation "Rally for the Cure"
Golf Tournament

Author's Notes

༦

I AM A NATIVE SON OF FLORENCE, ALABAMA, born, raised, and educated here. After starting my career in Florence with Blazer Finance, working opportunities with AmSouth, First Union, Wachovia, and Wells Fargo banks took me away from Florence for some forty-three years. I am now retired from the financial services industry, and returned home to Florence.

As stated in the book's introduction, until recently I had no idea how creatively successful Aunt Genett has been and thought to myself, her story must be told. Although I have written and published several books of different genres, this is my first attempt at writing a memoir type book and it has been an interesting and fun project.

I appreciate Aunt Genett's patience with me during the many interview sessions over the past six months, and her efforts to contact friends and former business associates. I thank family members for taking time to read the manuscript and the contributions they made to the book. I hope my writing and editing does justice to her success story, and you find it as fascinating as I did.

Charles E. Cabler
Shoals Writers Guild
Working Writers Club
Tennessee Valley Historical Society

Other books Charles has written
(Available through Amazon.com)

Create A Competitive Advantage

What Every Employee Should Know to Be Successful

Five Key Elements to Consider in Your Decision to Become a First Time Manager

The Chains of Marley-Our Christian and Humanitarian Benevolent Responsibility

(Available through the Old Buncombe County Genealogy Society, Ashville, North Carolina)
A History of the Baxter Cemetery-Camp Creek

Research and Reference Information

The Forks of Cypress photo credit, Wikipedia Encyclopedia web site- https://en.wikipedia.org

Log cabin photo credit, Library of Congress, Prints and Photographs Division, Washington, D.C.

Andrew Jackson land purchase reference-Florenceal.org Blog

Land purchase from Chief Double Head reference, The *North Alabama* Newspaper, summer, 1962 and web site- alabamapioneers.com

Information on James Jackson was excerpted from web site- wwwdeepfried-kudzu.com

Haley, Alex, *Queen: The Story of an American Family,* New edition 1993, Pan Books publisher

AARP magazine, April/May 2016, Loretta Lynn interview, Alanna Nash, staff writer

Stribling, T.S., *The Store,* 1932, Doubleday, Doran & Company Publishers

Times Daily Newspaper article, Top Billing, May 18, 2014, Teri Thornton, Lifestyle Editor

Bernina information extracted from web site -www.bernina.com/en-US-home-UnitedStates

Some New York trip information contributed by Anita Jaynes, Ruffles and Lace co-partner

Times Daily Newspaper article, Designing Women, September 9, 1998, Cathy Myers, staff writer

McCall's Pattern Magazine interview article, winter, 1990, Anne Marie Soto, writer

McCall's patterns # 8626, 9164, & 8885, The McCall Pattern Company, New York, New York

McCall's patterns #M 7311 and M 7343, The McCall Pattern Company, New York, New York

McCall's patterns #4206 and 4356, The McCall Pattern Company, New York, New York

Sales information provided by the McCall Pattern Company, New York City, New York

65494105R00061

Made in the USA
Charleston, SC
21 December 2016